About Demos

Demos is a greenhouse for new ideas which can improve the quality of our lives. As an independent think tank, we aim to create an open resource of knowledge and learning that operates beyond traditional party politics.

We connect researchers, thinkers and practitioners to an international network of people changing politics. Our ideas regularly influence government policy, but we also work with companies, NGOs, colleges and professional bodies.

Demos knowledge is organised around five themes, which combine to create new perspectives. The themes are democracy, learning, enterprise, quality of life and global change.

But we also understand that thinking by itself is not enough. Demos has helped to initiate a number of practical projects which are delivering real social benefit through the redesign of public services.

We bring together people from a wide range of backgrounds to cross-fertilise ideas and experience. By working with Demos, our partners develop a sharper insight into the way ideas shape society. For Demos, the process is as important as the final product.

www.demos.co.uk

First published in 2003
© Demos
Some rights reserved. See copyright licence for details

ISBN 1 84180 115 1
Typeset by Land & Unwin, Bugbrooke
Printed by Hendy Banks, London

For further information and
subscription details please contact:

Demos
The Mezzanine
Elizabeth House
39 York Road
London SE1 7NQ

telephone: 020 7401 5330
email: mail@demos.co.uk
web: www.demos.co.uk

The Adaptive State

Strategies for personalising
the public realm

Edited by
Tom Bentley
James Wilsdon

DEM⊖S

Contents

Acknowledgements

We would like to thank Hewlett-Packard for their generous support of this collection. Steve Gill, Paul Steels, Robert Watt and Tina Green at HP all contributed to the success of various stages of the project. Thanks also to Neal Lawson and David Abrahams at LLM for their advice and input throughout.

We are hugely grateful to all those whose essays, comments and feedback helped to shape the collection and its introduction: Jake Chapman, Bob Fryer, David Hargreaves, Ron Heifetz, Charles Leadbeater, Tony MacKay, Riel Miller, Robin Murray, Kate Oakley, Barry Quirk, Bob Tyrrell and Chris Yapp.

Several members of the Demos team also provided invaluable advice and support: John Craig, Claire Ghoussoub, Eddie Gibb, Matthew Horne, Lydia Howland, Helen McCarthy, Paul Miller, Sophia Parker, Paul Skidmore and Bobby Webster.

Tom Bentley and James Wilsdon
December 2003

Transforming public services
A Demos work programme

Demos is actively engaged in generating new ideas and strategies which can help public services adapt to a changing world. Through our work with organisations of every size and scale – from government departments to FTSE 100 companies, local authorities to charities – we have developed rich insights into what drives economic and social change, and how organisations can respond.

Our multidisciplinary approach to research and strategy enables us to work across policy, sectoral and disciplinary boundaries in a creative and imaginative way. We are experienced in the complexities of partnership working, and have undertaken numerous projects for public agencies, both in the UK and internationally.

Currently, our public sector partners include: Centrex; the Netherlands Ministry of Justice; the Department of Premier and Cabinet in Victoria, Australia; the National College for School Leadership; Creative Partnerships; Newcastle City Council; NHS University; the Department for Education and Skills; Neighbourhood Renewal Unit; Department for the Environment, Food and Rural Affairs; and the New Opportunities Fund.

By bridging the artificial divide between policy and practice, Demos has placed itself at the forefront of a new approach to transforming public services. Our aim is not only to generate new ideas through research and publications (see opposite), but also to create strategies through which new practices can merge. Core themes of our public services programme include:

- *Systems thinking* – this is a mature discipline in science and technology but is only now being applied to public policy-making, as a way of coping with complexity.
- *Networked learning* – fostering collaboration and knowledge-sharing between clusters of service organisations.
- *Personalisation* – constructing public service pathways designed around the profiles, capacities and motivations of individual users.
- *Leadership* – developing new leadership models for distributed capacity-building, and strategies for workforce development.
- *Public value* – identifying new methodologies which allow organisations to measure and enhance their contribution to the public realm.

We would be pleased to talk to organisations with a commitment to public service transformation.
For more information, please contact James Wilsdon, Head of Strategy (james@demos.co.uk ; +44 (0) 20 7401 5335)

Selected publications

Open Source Democracy · Douglas Rushkoff, 2003
Online, peer-to-peer communication have created new forms of interactions, which could revitalise democracy.

Education Epidemic · David Hargreaves, 2003
Instead of acting as hubs through which all new policies are routed, education departments must enable innovation networks to develop.

Beyond Measure · Paul Skidmore, 2003
The time has come to ditch the high stakes approach to school assessment which produces exam stress for all involved and fails to ensure improved performance.

People Flow · Theo Veenkamp, Alessandra Buonfino, Tom Bentley, 2003
Only by understanding the drivers for international people movement can a management system be developed to absorb the pressures they create.

Other People's Children · Gillian Thomas and Gina Hocking, 2003
Children have become 'invisible citizens' who live in a privatised world controlled increasingly by adults. A new agenda for children's quality of life is required.

Mobilisation · James Harkin, 2003
The next wave of mobile technologies could give rise to new location-based public services, and new forms of m-democracy.

Innovate from Within · Charles Leadbeater, 2002
Civil service reform is a prerequisite for transforming public services.

System Failure · Jake Chapman, 2002
The law of unintended consequences will always prevail in any attempt to change organisations by command or clever public policy instrument.

Classroom Assistance · Matthew Horne, 2001
The progressive transformation of the education system means harnessing the professional capabilities of teachers, and tackling recruitment problems in the process.

It's Democracy, Stupid · Tom Bentley, 2001
Political disengagement should not be mistaken for voter apathy; the public can be re-engaged by giving them a more direct role in democracy, or self-governance.

Foreword

Paul Steels

Public services matter to us as citizens, as members of our community and as the bedrock of business and economic success. The benefits of good education, high-performing healthcare, reliable local government and effective anti-crime measures are fundamental to a thriving society. In a world where risk is more and more individualised, the need for a public infrastructure that can underpin the common good is increasingly crucial.

But the ability of public services to deliver in a world of new opportunities, challenges and threats is being put to the test. People are less deferential and rightly demand greater accountability and higher quality of service. Choice is a given not an option, rights only come with responsibilities, and services are decentralising. Effectiveness is often found through the empowerment of citizens as co-producers. These dynamics are played out against a background where governments are struggling to maintain the trust of their citizens and continually have to demonstrate value for money.

The only constant is learning to live with change. How public service institutions and programmes adapt and learn to transform themselves from within is the critical challenge facing policy-makers, practitioners and public sector partners such as Hewlett-Packard (HP).

Following its recent merger with Compaq, HP has been a test case for successful transformation on a massive scale. At HP we know that technology can be a major enabler of change, if it is designed to support transformation as it develops. There are of course differences between the private and public sectors that have to be respected, but we can and must learn from each other.

Public services must be based on agile and adaptive platforms if they are to meet the challenges of continuous change. We are only now starting to learn what this means in practice, which is why this publication is tremendously helpful. It includes important contributions from the UK and across the world, from thinkers but also crucially from front-line practitioners. I am delighted that HP, working with Demos, has been able to make this contribution to thinking about the next stage of public service modernisation and renewal.

Paul Steels is director, public sector division, Hewlett-Packard.

1. Introduction

the adaptive state

Tom Bentley and James Wilsdon

> *Our new environment compels commitment and participation.*
> *We have become irrevocably involved with, and responsible for,*
> *each other.*
>
> *Marshall McLuhan, 1967*[1]

> *Even when a market is inappropriate, old command and control*
> *systems of management are not the way forward but, instead, we*
> *are seeking and should seek – in the NHS and other public*
> *services – a decentralised, not centralised, means of delivery*
> *compatible with equity and efficiency.*
>
> *Gordon Brown, 2003*[2]

Across the world, the quality of the public realm is now the central battleground of politics. For two decades, elections revolved around the competition for private wealth and individual freedoms. Today, our agendas are dominated by security, legitimacy and solidarity.[3] People want to know how government can help them face the uncertainties and insecurities that surround them. At a national level, the authority of public institutions is subject to increased scrutiny and pressure. In the international arena, dilemmas are framed by the interface between public legitimacy, personal belief and collective violence.

In this febrile atmosphere governments stand or fall on their effectiveness at renewing public goods. The task of reforming public services has become the most visible symbol of this wider challenge. In Britain, one of New Labour's greatest political achievements has been to shift the axis of domestic debate towards the quality and fairness of public service provision.

But efforts at building on this achievement have been undermined by a paradox. Measured by their own performance standards, there is no question that most public services in Britain have improved over the last six years. Yet nobody is satisfied. The 'invest and reform' message that defined New Labour's initial strategy is now widely acknowledged as insufficient.[4] So far, alternative promises to cut bureaucracy and extend individual choice do not add up to a widely convincing platform. As such, at a critical moment in the struggle to define the next period of politics, efforts to refresh the core services that voters regard as their priority have reached an impasse. Reformers are caught between the modesty of incremental improvement and the unpredictable effects of unconstrained diversity.

Two questions stand out. First, what will convince people that the quality and responsiveness of services has really improved? Second, how do existing reform strategies generate the legitimacy required to sustain more radical, ongoing change?

In this collection we argue that these questions can only be answered with a sharper moral and political vision of the role that public services play in people's lives. There is a need to revisit the purpose and shape of government itself, and explore models of organisational change for which the state is not currently equipped.

Radically different models of service, organisation and value are required. But these must also be compatible with the effort of sustaining and managing existing commitments in the here and now. As this collection shows, a set of principles, practices and strategies is emerging through which the simultaneous tasks of radical innovation and outcome improvement can be achieved. It remains to be seen which political party or set of institutions will make these new approaches its own. Welcome to the adaptive state.

Turning on a sixpence

All major parties are searching for formulas that offer their citizens security and reliability while also providing 'choice', 'diversity', 'flexibility' and 'responsiveness'. Political orthodoxy is also gathering around the need to devolve discretion closer to the front line. As Jackie Ashley has observed, 'If there were two buzz words which summed up the message from the 2003 party conference season they were "choice" and "localism". Everybody's spouting them.'[5]

But politicians everywhere are struggling to show how their promises convert into coherent action and tangible outcomes – that their particular version of the story can really be different from anybody else's. The problem is that the narrowness of the rhetorical space around public services restricts the range of organisational possibilities through which politicians can identify solutions. In an era where there are few clear-cut ideological alternatives, the moral and organisational principles underpinning reform remain foggy. The ideology of pragmatism gives rise to a 'pick and mix' approach to selecting policy tools and interventions.

All the main parties now recognise this challenge. And each is straining to establish its credentials as the natural home of the 'new localism'. For New Labour, several ministers have now acknowledged the limits of command-and-control approaches to reform.[6] For the Conservatives, Michael Howard used his inaugural speech as leader to reassure voters that he would 'cut the fly-by-wire controls that lead straight back to a dashboard in Whitehall . . . . Central control stifles initiative and innovation'.[7] And for the Liberal Democrats, Charles Kennedy has proposed scrapping five entire departments. His rationale: 'Save at the centre to get more help and services for people in the local community.'[8]

But this debate is being cast in the wrong terms. A false choice is on offer; a zero sum game between localism and central control, between diversity-through-choice and equity-through-standardisation. Both the advocates of the new localism and the defenders of centralism have missed an important dimension of the argument.[9] Successful reform does not only depend on the level and scale at which decisions are taken or performance is measured; it will require greater *adaptive capacity* in organisations at every level of the system.

Public services in diverse societies must offer far greater flexibility to meet personal needs, while keeping the ability to connect resources and activities across entire systems of governance. This is the only way to serve diverse needs equally well, and to make specialist knowledge and resources available to everybody. Services must also contribute to shared social contexts that enable people to thrive; performance within closed systems will be inadequate, however much improved.

In other words, we need systems capable of continuously reconfiguring themselves to create new sources of public value.[10] This means interactively linking the different layers and functions of governance, not searching for a static blueprint that predefines their relative weight. The central question is no longer how we can achieve precisely the right balance between different layers – central, regional and local – or between different sectors – public, private and voluntary. Instead, we need to ask *How can the system as a whole become more than the sum of its parts?*

This question casts present arguments over foundation hospitals or specialist schools in a slightly depressing light. Despite the importance of increasing the operational autonomy of provider organisations, the focus on rewarding above-average performance with formal permission to take a few more decisions seems a modest proposal. It certainly fails to justify the level of controversy that the proposed reforms have generated. With this kind of structural reform, gains in performance and innovation are likely to be constrained by the organisational models still implied by frameworks of accountability and measurement. As Jake Chapman argues in his essay, if new styles of management are developed without abandoning existing notions of control and predictability then the new styles will fail as surely as the old. 'Once the myth of control is abandoned then the debate about granting autonomy to hospitals is transformed – simply because control is recognised as not being an option.'[11]

State and society: reform versus innovation

Scientists working in the field of biodiversity have contrasted the
speed with which an iso-temperature line is moving northwards,
with the speed with which plants can naturally adapt and
migrate. So it is with public institutions. Left to themselves, can
they adapt as fast as the external environment is changing?[12]

Roughly once in every generation, a major question re-emerges about
the shape, effectiveness and legitimacy of the state. And every time, a
wave of reform seeks to adapt the existing structures of the state to
meet the needs and expectations of society in a better way. These
needs and expectations are themselves dynamic; driven and shaped,
though not predetermined, by wider patterns of innovation. As Chris
Freeman and Francisco Louca have shown, over the past two
centuries, five separate technological revolutions have successively
transformed the societies in which they were developed: water-
powered mechanisation; steam-powered mechanisation; electrifi-
cation; motorisation and computerisation. These can be understand
as long waves of innovation, growth and institutional change which
diffuse over time throughout whole societies.[13]

In the public sector, each burst of reform has sought to harness the
potential of innovation in other sectors in order to re-equip
government. In the mid and late nineteenth century, professionalism
and meritocracy updated the voluntaristic, ramshackle and
patronage-based model of administration. In the mid-twentieth
century, the principles of Fordist mass production were applied to
make welfare services universally available. During the 1970s and
1980s, neoliberalism offered a new mix of privatisation, agency-based
delivery and arms-length regulation. In the 1990s, the 'reinventing
government' agenda sought to import the tools of contract-based
accountability and performance management from the private sector.

The current approach to reform therefore rests on a curious
hybrid, combining:

○ the nineteenth-century liberal administrative state, embodied in central government departments and local authority structures, and the model of financial accountability represented by Parliament's public accounts committee

○ the postwar welfare state, which introduced mass-production service management and procurement, from universal schooling to the NHS

○ the neoliberal legacy of agencies, performance indicators, contract-based accountability and arms-length public bodies

○ the performance culture of modern public sector management, a unique and intriguing mix of mandarin wisdom and 1980s business performance techniques.

The effort to improve performance raises the question of how to make the state itself more effective, rather than simply bigger or smaller, more centralised or localised. The danger, however, is that in the rush to find means of improvement the wrong set of external innovations and techniques becomes the basis for new strategies. It is all too easy to neglect the assumptions and beliefs that lie submerged beneath the surface of government, what Mary Midgley describes as the 'philosophical plumbing' of any system or organisation.[14] Yet it is often these hidden choices, and the powerful cultures that they give rise to, which determine the prospects of radically better outcomes.

So, while government and public services certainly need to import new practices, innovations and tools developed elsewhere, there may also be a great deal to learn from their own extraordinary resilience. Public institutions, from the central civil service to the local school, have adapted repeatedly to changing conditions in ways that have preserved their core internal values and underpinning structures. Despite decades of reform, we still have a health service organised through hospitals, GP practices and professions. Even in towns and cities where services have failed chronically over a generation, local councils and other civic institutions have survived.

If citizens are to thrive in the same way, they need more of this adaptive capacity in order to achieve the right outcomes for their lives. The challenge is to harness the adaptive potential of public organisation more directly to the task of creating public value. And the way to do this is by linking processes of organisational change, within and beyond the formal boundaries of the public sector, more closely to positive outcomes. Government must absorb new capabilities to achieve this. But it must also turn itself inside out, becoming more responsive and connected to the distributed processes through which social outcomes are actually generated.

Universal personalisation

This massive reorientation of government cannot be accomplished without a clear moral and political vision. Despite its commitment to public services, New Labour has so far failed to provide this compelling, long-term vision. The myriad efforts to improve and 'modernise' too often look like hyperactivity without purpose. In part, this is because New Labour has taken the function of services for granted and built improvement strategies around 'common sense' definitions of performance, which are only indirectly related to the outcome values of public service investment. Hospital waiting lists, and even the new focus on waiting times, are only a proxy measure for public satisfaction with health outcomes. Reducing class sizes only makes sense if the organisational context of schooling is already fixed and standardised.

Public services matter because they can provide a sense of security and solidarity, a partial sanctuary from exposure to the global marketplace. We all depend on public services, not only to meet our concrete individual needs, but to provide a space in which everyday social interactions occur – in parks, libraries and playgrounds, or through improved housing and support during major life events like pregnancy or retirement.

But as society becomes more diverse, personal aspirations are changing. Describing the modern corporation, Shoshana Zuboff and James Maxmin observe that 'People have changed more than the business organisations upon which they depend…The chasm that now separates individuals and organisations is marked by frustration, mistrust, disappointment and even rage'.[15] If this applies to companies – usually perceived as highly responsive to consumer needs – how much more so does it apply to public services?

As our aspirations change and diversify, we increasingly want a form of connection to the public realm that reflects our outlook and circumstances. We still rely on a shared social context that is bigger than ourselves, but we are less ready to submit to standardised relationships with large, impersonal organisations. The more we learn about the factors shaping mobility, achievement, and wellbeing, the clearer it becomes that services that genuinely engage with the particular needs of users are more effective in creating positive outcomes. To use resources effectively, services must be personalised. But for the experience of personalised public services to meet and reinforce shared expectations and principles of social justice, they must also be genuinely universal.

This is the vision that politics should offer; of a public realm that treats each individual as having equal worth by adapting its support to their unique needs and potential. But having evolved through the frames of mass production and contract-based accountability, how can the myriad forms of public service develop the capacity to offer this kind of personalised experience to users?

The key to unlocking this potential is the recognition that public value is created, not delivered.[16] As Patricia Hewitt has admitted, in this context it may have been a mistake to stress 'delivery, delivery, delivery' as Labour's second term priority for public service reform: 'You actually can't deliver good health or safe streets in the way that commercial companies can deliver pizzas.'[17] Solutions rely, at least in part, on the users themselves, and their capacity to take shared responsibility for positive outcomes. In learning, health, work, and even parenting, positive outcomes arise from a combination of personal effort and wider social resources. An implicit understanding of this is already built into the way we behave. For example, the competition for places at popular schools is based on a tacit understanding that learning is co-produced, not only by pupils and their teachers, but by pupils and their peers.

The challenge is how to define more systematically the processes of 'co-production' through which public value is created, and then to connect different co-production activities to generate economies of scale and wider systems of support. For this to occur, we need to move beyond the negative definitions of Beveridge's welfare state, which saw public services as the means to eradicate 'evils' from public life, towards a set of positive outcomes. The time is now right to replace Beveridge's five giants – want, disease, ignorance, idleness and squalor – with five core dimensions of wellbeing for the early twenty-first century:

O shelter
O nurture
O learning
O health
O work and livelihood.

These arise from the same basic human needs. But they can be expressed as positive aspirations that are dynamic and take many forms. The quality and definition of these public goods are constantly evolving, and public service organisation must continuously adapt to meet them. For example, personalised health care requires treatment pathways that apply the best available knowledge about clinical effectiveness to the profile of the individual patient. But it also means making medical and care support available in a way that comple-ments home care and family needs. And it means addressing the environmental and behavioural factors that impact on health and wellbeing. As Anna Coote has argued, the government 'needs to open up a new kind of dialogue with the electorate about what health means, how it is secured and what to expect from others, including the NHS...this new conversation would aim to develop a wider understanding that health is not something we get from the NHS, but a resource that we and our fellow citizens own and must nurture and protect'.[18]

In education, personalisation means constructing pathways through a flexible curriculum, which is crafted to reflect the intelligences and capacities of the individual learner. But it also means linking the professional input of teachers and mentors to wider sources of support for independent learning. In a forthcoming Demos pamphlet, Charles Leadbeater describes personalisation as 'rewriting the scripts' of public services. 'At the moment, most children in this country have their education fitted into a standardised script of stages and tests...Personalised learning needs to provide children with a far greater repertoire of possible scripts for how their education unfolds.'[19] The script for personalised learning would be based on the user being far more active in determining their own timeline for learning, involving a mix of ingredients that suits their aspirations and abilities.

Personalisation means far more than being able to choose between different service suppliers. It requires services to be actively shaped in response to individual profiles. This does not mean separate, isolated programmes; many of the activities involved in being healthy or learning effectively are collaborative and intensively social. But it does mean that provider organisations must be capable of adapting and reconfiguring what they offer to ensure that it fits the profile of individual needs. This in turn requires structures of governance, resourcing and accountability that reward improved outcomes and support the flexibility required to offer personalisation on a mass scale.

Beyond factory re-engineering

Each large system of public services contains huge variations in performance and effectiveness. Each generates a spectrum of innovations, ranging from incremental to revolutionary. The current reform programme employs a panoply of methods, from workaday improvements to the creation of entirely new services and delivery channels. But the dominant paradigm of organisation remains an 'input–process–output' model, which regards 'performance management' and formal restructuring as the main avenues to better outcomes.[20]

The current preoccupation with setting national standards as a basis for accountability obscures a tension that the process of adaptive reform must address; the specification of performance standards often narrows the scope for organisational innovation. This is partly because it encourages risk aversion, but more importantly because it establishes rigid parameters of organisation and formal responsibility. In fact, some of the most significant performance gains may arise from cross-boundary collaboration – something that is hard to design into the formal functions of bounded organisations. This does not mean that targets and standards are not essential. But they must be used judiciously, and owned by the participants, rather than used primarily as an instrument of control.

The same applies to the process of restructuring. Often this can be necessary to achieve new objectives and develop new capabilities. But anyone who has lived through a restructuring process knows that organisations do not stick to the formal specifications of their redesign for very long – the processes and relationships that hold them together are far more complex and powerful, and cannot easily be transformed by a new organogram.

So why is restructuring such a popular solution? The simple answer is that the formal structures and functions of organisations are one of the relatively few aspects of organisational performance that politicians and administrators hold directly in their hands. Restructuring is often presented as a straightforward solution to a complex problem. Take the recent example of Lord Haskins' review of rural services. Although Haskins is probably correct in identifying the need for better integration between rural delivery agencies, his proposed solution – combining English Nature, the Rural Development Service and parts of the Countryside agency into a new super-agency – seems likely to be a recipe for five more years of organisational chaos and inertia.[21]

Think tanks too must bear some responsibility for this tendency. Bold calls for institutional redesign are too often the refuge of the lazy pamphleteer. Such proposals frequently obscure as much as they illuminate the real causes of improved performance. Process re-engineering cannot by itself generate more capacity for mass personalisation because the methods of planning and resource allocation used in the frameworks of public accountability no longer work in complex operational environments. As the growing problem of unintended consequences shows, command and control methods are incapable of coordination over any significant period of time. Organisations, especially those responding to local pressures, already rely on other patterns of response in order to solve problems as they arise.

In all major areas of public policy Whitehall departments must contend with highly distributed fields of organisation, which spread beyond formal lines of control. The Department of Work and Pensions has a client base of millions, and seeks to influence the behaviour of thousands of financial service providers. The NHS is a vast, heaving ecology of interlinked organisations and groups. The criminal justice system consists of many different agencies with separate cultures, histories and incentives, all striving to operate as part of a single system.

The reality with which all governments are struggling is the uncontrollable, dynamic nature of human activity. The success of modern capitalism in generating wealth and choice for most people, and of earlier social reforms in improving their levels of health and education, have helped to create demands that are increasingly diverse in their expression. Not only do these demands require more sophisticated responses, but they also contain the seeds of future demands – the more access to knowledge and learning we have, for example, the more likely we are to seek more of it.

From a patient's perspective, the range of influences that affect personal health is not bounded by the framework of 'clinical governance' or the standard procedures for diagnosis and treatment. For the school student, most of whose time and attention are devoted to situations other than lessons, the forms of knowledge that can influence their learning and aspirations are far more extensive than those which are channelled through the formal curriculum. For the commuter, the reliability and cost of a public transport system are only one factor influencing their means of travel and the way they structure their journey.

In each of these cases, and in many more, the factors influencing our efforts to achieve an outcome are varied and unpredictable. The consequences of these processes can be unintended and counter-intuitive. For example, a concerted effort to drive down street crime may have the unintended effect of displacing some forms of criminal activity into other areas. The decision to raise National Insurance contributions in order to fund public services may have a knock-on effect on teachers' salary costs, which unintentionally makes it harder for schools to balance their budgets. The decision to incentivise rail service providers to maximise the number of services may create new pressures on the crumbling rail infrastructure.

The point is not just that individual policy decisions will produce a range of effects that far-sighted policy-makers ought to anticipate, but that the interconnections between different systems make it inevitable that use and need will follow unpredictable patterns. Public service providers will always be faced with a continuous evolution of demand. Equally, the interconnections between different aspects of life can mean that the pressures on public service organisations arise from shifts elsewhere in society. So, for example, growing stress in working life may impact negatively on the demand for health services. Changing working hours may make it increasingly difficult for parents to ensure their children's readiness for school.

Diversity and complexity make it more difficult to govern services through hierarchical coordination. Yet this basic method still lies at the heart of our conception of government, and conditions the behaviour of politicians, regulators, managers and professionals. Across the public sector, as Jake Chapman points out, mental models have been based on the use of mechanistic metaphors: 'Phrases such as "the machinery of government", "driving through change", "stepping up a gear" and "policy levers" are all based on images of machines.'[22]

Principles of adaptive organisation

In these complex circumstances, people and organisations have to become adaptive. Something is said to be adaptive when it responds to changes in its environment without central direction or control, while retaining some core structure or values.[23]

Beehives are an interesting example. For many years, biologists assumed that the queen bee directed all the other bees and coordinated the hive. In fact, the key to the hive's success lies in the fact that no individual bee has to understand the system. Rather than awaiting orders, bees pay attention to their neighbours to decide what to do next. As a result, hives successfully feed and protect themselves, evolving as they go.[24]

It is a central argument of this collection that public services should be understood as complex adaptive systems and not according to the mechanistic models that have traditionally dominated government thinking. Paul Plsek likens this difference to that between throwing a stone and throwing a live bird. The trajectory of the stone can be calculated precisely using the laws of physics. The trajectory of the bird is far less predictable.[25]

The question is whether policy-makers can embrace this shift in perspective, and redefine their role as supporters of adaptive processes of change. They need to stop pretending they are throwing stones, and acknowledge that the management of public services is far more akin to throwing birds. Such a shift would require government to become adept at shaping diverse sets of activities and providers, regardless of whether they are introduced through market competition. A capacity to enable 'disciplined innovation', where the discipline is a relentless quest to create new manifestations of public value, would become the central challenge.

There are many possible routes through which progress towards an adaptive state is possible. The essays in this collection illustrate several viable elements of a new, dynamic settlement. For us, eight principles stand out as fundamental to the formation of adaptive governance systems.

1. *Accountability for learning* The principle of formal
    accountability for public spending remains fundamental.
    But there is no reason why vertical accountability systems
    should stand in the way of greater flexibility and
    adaptability. As Riel Miller argues in Chapter 9, there are
    many ways in which governments can encourage learning
    through experimentation. Alongside the need for probity
    and transparency in the use of public funds, public
    servants should also be able to account for their
    responsiveness to what can be learned from multiple
    efforts to innovate and improve effectiveness.

2. *Open governance* Learning, adaptability and flexible
    coordination are encouraged by transparency. Too many
    management and policy functions are still shrouded in
    institutional mystery for reasons of tradition and culture.
    The design of governance structures should reflect the
    values of openness and transparency as the basis of a new
    generation of organisational templates. Open innovation
    strategies treat the whole field of practice as a base for
    generating useful innovations, rather than treating
    innovation as a specialised supply line with fixed points of
    entry into strategic decision-making.

3. *Modular innovation* As Charles Leadbeater demonstrates
    in Chapter 2, modularity provides a way for organisations
    to gain the benefits of scale and specialisation without
    succumbing to unnecessary standardisation or
    fragmentation. Adaptive organisations need to delegate
    responsibility for specific outcomes and link these
    through clear rules of interaction and interoperability.

4. *Richer analytical frameworks* Government should be able
    to draw on a far richer repertoire of conceptual models
    and analytical techniques in undertaking policy develop-
    ment and implementation processes. As Jake Chapman

argues in Chapter 3, systems thinking and futures methodologies should become part of the standard repertoire of skills development and management training in all large public agencies. In Chapter 7, Kate Oakley makes the case for new forms of local knowledge and a greater recognition of the value of that knowledge by central government.

5. *Participation by design* Public services need to be developed through interactive processes that give practitioners and users a direct role in shaping the end result. Experimentation with participative processes should be given equal priority to the current emphasis on the speed and economy of implementation. The planning of public spaces and public buildings, such as schools and hospitals, should be undertaken with user participation as a central dimension of the development process.[26] As Barry Quirk describes in Chapter 8, local authorities are ideally placed to pioneer these new approaches.

6. *Interdependence through networks* Positive interdependence between groups of service organisations and policy-making bodies should be fostered through the creation of knowledge sharing and learning networks. 'Open source' approaches to sharing strategies for innovation and effectiveness should become a staple part of professional development, audit and evaluation. In Chapter 6, David Hargreaves outlines how this can be applied within the education system. And in Chapter 11, Robert Watt describes the role that technology can play in enabling networked approaches to transformation.

7. *Prioritising people* The need for adaptive organisations reinforces the urgency of avoiding any drift towards a two-tier workforce. As Bob Fryer argues in Chapter 4, workforce reform should place greater emphasis on

learning and skills development, increase the scope for
lateral progression of public service workers through a
range of roles and organisations, and create more
opportunities for career progression, irrespective of skill
base or starting point.

8. *Leadership for public value* Adaptive change demands
sustained leadership of particular kinds. As Ron Heifetz
argues in Chapter 5, a new generation of leadership
strategies for distributed capacity-building is needed
across the public services. This needs to take place
simultaneously in political, public service and community
roles in order to have a cumulative impact. Adaptive
leadership enables fragmented constituencies to mobilise
around common objectives; a prerequisite for focusing
reform and adaptation around challenging outcomes.

Identifying a set of immediate priorities

The analysis in this collection does not lead directly to traditional
policy prescriptions, in part because it suggests that the structural
separation between policy and implementation is one of the barriers
to system-wide transformation. Rather than defining a new set of
measures to be implemented through the familiar model of linear
change, we need a set of priorities and strategic approaches that can
help to increase the spread of excellence and adaptive capacity.

Strengthening this adaptive capacity, and linking it directly to the
creation of public value, is a priority that can be applied to existing
systems and policies. This requires strategies to amplify the value of
localised effectiveness and excellence, and to encourage its rapid
spread across larger national or regional systems of health, education,
welfare and business support. Several priorities do stand out,
however, as having universal relevance and urgency.

First, there is a need to incorporate public value objectives directly
into the performance goals and accountability systems of all service
providers. This means there must be a renewed focus on outcome

indicators and the ways they are collected, and techniques that could put outcome information directly in the hands of users and practitioners, instead of it landing on the desks of policy professionals, academics and auditors.

Second, the debate about control and autonomy must not purely be focused on the formal autonomy of public service organisations in relation to central government. Self-governance is another important dimension of autonomy that public services should display, which is rooted in the ability of people and communities to shape their own priorities. They cannot do this without the support of a responsive public realm, constituted in large part by the rich ecology of public organisations and resources.

Third, the central focus of the 'capacity-building' agenda, which is already gaining momentum, must not be power, money or organisational models, but knowledge and learning. Effective organisations mobilise resources through the creation and application of practical know-how. They become effective in their field through an ongoing process of learning, which, in the most inspiring organisations, becomes embedded in their culture. National institutions need new ways to learn from the evolutionary processes through which local service organisations develop their capacity.

Fourth, the strategic use of networks is probably the most compelling opportunity for reformers to accelerate positive change. Networks can underpin the lateral transfer of innovation, support cultures of mutual accountability, and enable the clustering of delivery organisations. Networks are also a strong feature of the 'collaborative governance' models through which more responsive and transparent local systems could evolve. Successful experiments are already under way; for example, NHS collaboratives allow networks of clinical practitioners to exchange and refine ideas about how to solve common problems, such as the improvement of cancer or coronary care. They spread the best knowledge available through a series of lateral 'waves' rather than through hierarchical structures.

Fifth, demand is the root of radical change. Supply side reform, however serious or inspired, will not generate the responsiveness that every politician now feels compelled to offer. Personalisation is pivotal to effective public services because it offers individuals the chance to shape the course and outcome of their public service experience. Only by sharing the power to allocate and sequence organisational resources will public services be able to legitimise the investment they represent. This will often mean choice by consumers between different suppliers and delivery channels. But, more importantly, it means letting the voice and behaviour of everyday service users drive the reform efforts of local public institutions.[27]

In search of politics

This entire process must be led by politics. Politicians have a formative responsibility to reflect public aspirations and project new possibilities. The challenge for them is to focus the next stage of public debate on the social outcomes to which reform should be addressed, without reaching too fast for rigid definitions of performance or tools of intervention that restrict the potential for adaptive self-governance. As several of our authors point out, the outcomes and values that public organisations create will often conflict. Politics is the arena in which those conflicts and choices should be played out.

Our current definitions of successful political leadership require elected politicians to grapple with a level of organisational detail and overload that is unsustainable. Nye Bevan once famously said that the sound of a bedpan dropped on an NHS ward would reverberate around Whitehall. Today, despite the rhetoric of the new localism, too many ministers remain seduced by Bevanite myths of omniscience and control. The reality is that they cannot be in control of the organisational systems that they nominally head, even though they retain responsibility for them.

So what practical steps could politicians and others take to realise the vision of the adaptive state? Politicians could:

O   focus their commitments on outcome goals that go
       beyond the output targets of existing organisations;

goals such as eliminating child poverty, reducing obesity, increasing the quality of working life, and giving every child the capacity and motivation to learn successfully

O   acknowledge the limits of their powers, and focus on mobilising wider constituencies for change

O   champion more radical forms of bureaucratic renewal by resisting the pressure to launch interventions through existing structures, and mandating a smaller, more agile and transparent civil service

O   learn and champion new skills and methods for sustaining organisational change and promoting accountability

O   create an expectation that direct user participation is a required feature of the design, delivery and evaluation of public services and public infrastructure.

The civil service could:

O   be bolder in acknowledging the extent of institutional renewal needed for effective government in the twenty-first century

O   develop a broader range of learning and modelling techniques with which to diagnose and shape the management of complex systems

O   promote cross-functional and team-based learning, and make a fundamental commitment to greater transparency in organisation and culture

O   develop clearer distinctions between the different skill sets required for policy development, strategic and project management, evaluation and organisational learning, innovation and cultural change, procurement and contract negotiation

O   learn and share more systematically across the experiences of parallel efforts in different countries.

National policy could:

O incorporate public value measures and indicators, including levels of trust and wellbeing, into the regulatory frameworks for audit and inspection

O create formal accountability for learning, by requiring national agencies and departments to share transparently how they seek to learn from the wider systems they are responsible for

O dedicate ICT and e-government investment to creating a supportive infrastructure for lateral knowledge transfer between delivery organisations and citizens

O reshape research and development frameworks to prioritise distributed innovation and real-time, user-led forms of knowledge alongside the evidence and technical knowledge currently emphasised

O accelerate the shift in information policy towards providing local as well as national aggregated datasets, covering a wide range of wellbeing and outcome indicators, which can act as tools and resources for public service providers.

Audit and improvement agencies could:

O review and adapt their methods of data collection and intervention with the aim of supporting the continuous self-evaluation and peer review of delivery organisations

O strengthen their own peer review networks and promote more open debate about the commonalities and limitations of the methods used by different inspectorates in different sectors and industries

O investigate and deepen their understanding of the conditions under which practitioners and service users actually use the information created by inspection and audit

- ○ develop frameworks for modelling and inspecting collaborative and interdependent networks and systems of organisation.

Public service practitioners could:

- ○ expose themselves to a wider range of organisational environments and methods of practice
- ○ lead the formation of new civic and community networks
- ○ experiment with new team-based and modular structures within their organisations
- ○ undertake knowledge and network audits to identify and redirect their existing stocks of adaptive and innovative capacity.

Towards the adaptive state?

At no point in the modern history of public services have there been more resources, or a better range of tools, to use in the creation of public value. But if public services are going to achieve their full potential over the next generation, they must be reshaped through an open, evolutionary process. This process will not arise from the perpetual efforts to restructure existing arrangements, without changing the dominant assumptions governing models of organisation. The opportunity now exists for systems that are flexible enough to personalise everything they offer, and responsive to the public they serve. To get the public services we deserve, 'modernisation' must acquire a new meaning. In the long run, adaptability matters more than performance within rigid boundaries, so long as it can be shaped towards better life outcomes for everybody. The challenge is to give practical momentum to this agenda amid the noise and pressure of tomorrow's demands.

Tom Bentley is director of Demos and James Wilsdon is head of strategy.

Notes

1   M McLuhan and Q Fiore, *The Medium is the Message: an inventory of effects* (New York: Bantam, 1967).
2   Speech to the Social Market Foundation, 3 Feb 2003.
3   As Albert Hirschman notes in *The Passion and the Interests* (Princeton University Press, 1992), politics tends to swing through 30-year cycles of public versus private concerns.
4   See for example the recent Compass statement (www.compassonline.org.uk), and speeches by Alan Milburn and Stephen Byers.
5   J Ashley, 'Three parties, but just one reactionary mantra', *Guardian*, 11 Oct 2003.
6   See for example, Gordon Brown's speech to the Social Market Foundation, 3 Feb 2003, and John Reid's speech to the New Health Network, 15 July 2003.
7   Leadership acceptance speech, 6 Nov 2003.
8   Party conference speech, 25 Sept 2003.
9   D Corry and G Stoker, *New Localism: refashioning the centre-local relationship* (London: New Local Government Network, 2002); D Walker, *In Praise of Centralism: a critique of the new localism* (London: Catalyst, 2002).
10 The Strategy Unit in the Cabinet Office defines public value as 'an attempt to measure the total benefits which flow from government action'. For a fuller account, see G Kelly and S Muers, *Creating Public Value: an analytical framework for public service reform* (London: Cabinet Office, 2002), or Jake Chapman's essay in Chapter 10 of this collection.
11 See Chapter 3 of this collection.
12 Sir Andrew Turnbull, 'Beyond Sir Humphrey: reform and innovation in public administration in the 21st century', Speech in Portugal, 23 Oct 2003.
13 C Freeman and F Louca, *As Time Goes By: from the industrial revolutions to the information revolution* (Oxford: OUP, 2001).
14 M Midgley, *Utopias, Dolphins and Computers* (London: Routledge, 1996).
15 S Zuboff and J Maxmin, *The Support Economy: why corporations are failing individuals and the next episode of capitalism* (London: Penguin, 2002).
16 M H Moore, *Creating Public Value: strategic management in government* (Cambridge, Mass.: Harvard University Press, 1995); C Leadbeater, *The Man in the Caravan* (London: IDEA, 2003).
17 M White, 'We got it wrong, admits Blair', *Guardian*, 5 July 2003.
18 A Coote, 'A fourth way for health policy', *Renewal* 11 no 3 (2003).
19 C Leadbeater, *Personalisation through Participation* (London: Demos, forthcoming, 2004).
20 D Hargreaves, *Education Epidemic: transforming secondary schools through innovation networks* (London: Demos, 2003).
21 C Haskins, *Rural Delivery Review: a report on the delivery of government policies in rural England* (London: Defra, October 2003).
22 See Chapter 3 of this collection.
23 J Chapman, *System Failure: why governments must learn to think differently* (London: Demos, 2002).

24   J Jacobs, *The Nature of Economies*, (New York: Vintage Books, 2001).

25   P Plsek, 'Why won't the NHS do as it's told', plenary address, NHS Conference, July 2001.

26   Projects such as School Works are an excellent example of this type of participatory design (www.school-works.org).

27   C Leadbeater, *Personalisation through Participation*, (London: Demos, forthcoming, 2004).

2. Open innovation in public services

Charles Leadbeater

Ros McMullen starts her day as head of Kingsdown Secondary School in Wigan at 8.30am by wolfing down a bowl of Weetabix, before meeting the family of an Albanian asylum seeker who has just joined her school. There is no let-up: problems, challenges, decisions come thick and fast throughout the day. Yet McMullen has imposed a basic kind of order on an unruly and occasionally chaotic environment, thanks to a homegrown form of innovation.[1]

When McMullen took over Kingsdown in September 2000 its GCSE results meant that it was one of the worst secondary schools in the country. She came in with a team of three advisory heads who were on loan one day a week from their own schools elsewhere in Wigan. Their collaborative approach allowed McMullen to focus on the 'front of house' job of discipline, attendance and teaching quality, while the other heads set about putting the finances, curriculum and staffing structures right. They reckon they managed to do two years' work in less than six months, dramatically accelerating Kingsdown's improvement.

At roughly the same time that McMullen starts work David Miliband, the schools minister, is sitting at his desk in Whitehall, talking to his officials about plans they have that could change the way the entire secondary school system works. Miliband is another innovator: he wants to find ways to marshal the capabilities of the system as a whole to deliver better educational outcomes.

One of the key challenges facing the public sector is how best to connect McMullen and Miliband: how to link innovation at the grass roots with innovation that changes the entire system.

Too much innovation of the wrong kind

Left to her own devices, McMullen would continue to generate significant improvements for the kids at her school, most of whom come from run-down housing estates. The case for allowing more local solutions in public services, tailored to local needs and mobilising locally available talent and resources, is hugely powerful. Despite their best intentions, civil servants and politicians in Whitehall do not have the knowledge and drive to find a solution to Kingsdown's difficulties. Kingsdown needs to devise its own way forward: improvement cannot be delivered from on high, it can only be created in situ. If each of our more than 3,000 secondary schools were innovating like Kingsdown, the public sector would have a vast portfolio of experiments and potential solutions available to it.

Yet McMullen cannot innovate in a vacuum. Some of her ideas have come from other schools. Her freedom and incentives to innovate are vitally affected by national policy. There is a danger in any system of having too much decentralised innovation, which can lead to fragmentation and parochialism. All too often good ideas remain trapped in their local niche. Worse, local loyalties often mean that people resist ideas from outside. The nineteenth- and early twentieth-century welfare and education systems, which thrived on local and voluntary initiative, were ramshackle, fragmented and highly variable in quality. It was precisely these failings that paved the way for the state's growing role in the twentieth century.

To avoid parochialism and fragmentation the public sector needs decentralised innovation that has a cumulative effect on the system as a whole. Moves towards more decentralisation and 'new localism' need to be matched by mechanisms to propagate and spread good ideas, allowing them to reproduce and mutate in the process.

An understandable response to the challenge of propagation is to turn to the centre to legitimise and spread system-wide innovation, in the form of policies, guidance notes, instructions and targets. Most innovative organisations and networks have a strong centre which integrates knowledge, establishes common standards and identifies strategic challenges. Open and porous boundaries, which allow ideas to be exchanged with the outside world, are combined with strong, entrepreneurial centres.

Central initiative is now widely derided as 'command and control'. This is far too sweeping. Some degree of overall architecture is vital to keep a system together and developing as a whole. The problem is that the good intentions of people at the centre are often unintentionally thwarted because they get turned into crude and mechanistic targets, restrictions and instructions which undermine local initiative. That in turn creates a self-defeating spiral of diminishing returns in which the centre pushes harder to get results, with more targets, penalties and inspections, thus only increasing resentment among local providers.

The British public sector not only needs more decentralisation but also a different role for the centre, so that it is better able to look after system-wide innovation. This will require the centre to rethink radically and move away from the mechanistic models of change – target, incentives, inspection and penalties – that it currently works with.

Getting the mix right

Yet the problem with the British public sector is not that there is too little innovation and adaptation. On the contrary, there is too much innovation of the wrong kind, as we swing between high-risk, system-wide changes dreamt up at the centre – comprehensives, AS-levels and nursery vouchers – and masses of decentralised innovation which remains trapped on location.

The challenge is to find a way to create coherent, widespread innovation in distributed and complex systems, in which there are many players whom the government can direct only at great cost. Government has to learn how to influence these distributed systems without trying to control every detail of their operation.

More problematic still, our public services are distributed and networked systems with peculiar characteristics. In computing and other high technology industries, networks are characterised by high levels of innovation and new entry from start-up companies challenging incumbents. But in public services competition is limited and consumers have a restricted choice of providers. In the IT industry, the feedback loops are very fast. Once an innovation is launched it takes only a few months to work out whether it's going to be a flop: learning is rapid. In the public sector, it takes many years for an innovation to be a proven success or failure: learning is very slow.

This then is the challenge for an adaptive public sector: promoting innovation in services such as education and health to raise standards for all users, while recognising that these services depend on a highly distributed network of providers, in which there is limited new entry, competition and choice and where learning from innovation takes an enormously long time.

Where we should we look for clues to try to solve this intractable problem?

Open communities of innovation

The most promising solutions to this conundrum are emerging from open communities of innovation in high technology industries, the most famous of which is perhaps the Linux open source software programming community.[2]

Linux started when Linus Torvalds, a Finnish programmer, posted the core to his proposed computer operating system on the internet, inviting other programmers to make improvements. Hundreds of programmers began to join in, proposing amendments, additions and deletions. Together they created a community of innovation, around the Linux programme, which is now so robust that it is used widely in business.

Linux is not a one-off case. Another software programme created by an open source community runs the Strategic Rail Authority's website and most internet servers run on Apache, a programme created by an open source community. Indeed Linux represents a new model for open, networked innovation, which combines three ingredients:

o *Modularity* The programme could be broken down into sub-systems, so that innovators could focus on particular modules without having to change the entire system. That allowed multiple and parallel efforts at innovation to take place simultaneously.

o *Open standards* Torvalds set clear standards against which proposed innovations could be judged. The source code for the programme was left open for innovators to examine and modify. This meant that information could be readily shared among many developers but their efforts could be fairly judged against a publicly visible yardstick.

o *Central design authority* Torvalds kept control of the kernel of the Linux programme and was the final arbiter of changes to the kernel. The community had an authoritative leader.

Open communities of innovation like Linux seem to combine many ingredients that are traditionally kept separate, or at least prove difficult to combine. There is healthy competition within the community but also cooperation and sharing; it thrives on masses of individual initiative but is founded on a public good, the open source code left on the internet; the community is highly distributed and virtual, yet also hierarchical, with a single authority at its heart. As a result, decentralised efforts at innovation are also integrated at the core. A cacophony of localised innovation cumulates to create system-wide change.

Open innovation in organisations

Partly in response to these open communities of innovation, large companies are also shifting from closed to open models of innovation, designed to allow them to take advantage of new ideas emerging outside the organisation, whether from suppliers, partners, competitors or consumers.[3]

For much of the twentieth century large companies thought of innovation as a pipeline that started with research and development in large labs and fed through to manufacturing, market and sales. The emphasis was on hiring bright people, investing in research, keeping knowledge within the company, and protecting intellectual property through patents.

In fast-moving industries where new technologies are emerging the whole time, however, even large companies are shifting from closed, internally driven innovation to open, networked approaches. The role of internal research and development is increasingly to allow the company to engage with a wide array of external ideas that might be emerging in universities, start-up companies or competitors. By working with a wide range of external developers, an open innovator can plug into multiple experiments and innovations. External developers might also explore different routes to take a product to market. Done in the right way, open innovation increases the 'metabolic rate' at which companies generate, test and adopt ideas.

An outstanding example of open innovation is Intel's Architecture Lab, which the company created to orchestrate its work with communities of external developers. Intel reasoned that demand for its product – microprocessors – would only increase if there was a flow of applications and devices that drove demand for computers. So it set out to work with the developers of those applications. Sin Lin Chou of Intel explains:

> *Our primary role is to link Intel into the outside research community. We need to do enough internal work to be knowledgeable enough to talk with outside developers and to know which approaches might be most promising. We also need enough internal knowledge to be able to transfer promising research back inside Intel quickly.*

What would it take to develop an open innovation model for the public sector in which the role of the centre was like that of Linus Torvalds in Linux or the Intel Architecture Lab: promoting multiple efforts at decentralised, external innovation and then integrating promising ideas into the system as a whole? A starting point is to promote the idea of modularity.

Modularity

Fred Beck had a problem. Beck was in charge of developing IBM's System 360 computer in 1964. He wanted everyone involved to be kept abreast of what everyone else was doing. Daily notes of changes to aspects of the system were shared with everyone. Pretty soon most people on the project started their day sifting through a two-inch thick wad of notes. Just handling the information was becoming a major task in itself. As the complexity of the product increased, so the division of labour expanded, with more and more subgroups. Coordinating these different groups then required such volumes of information that people were left drowning in it. The complexity of the project meant that costs of communication and coordination spiralled out of control.[4]

By the time the project workbook detailing all the cumulative changes was five feet long, Beck decided he needed a change of tack. His innovation was one of design and organisation but its impact on the computer industry was as far-reaching as any technological innovation. He decided to break down the S360 into discrete modules that could be worked on separately. A core team set and maintained some visible, central design rules which specified the interfaces between the modules to make sure they all fitted together to form a whole. But the teams designing different modules did not have to know in detail what the others were doing.

The combination of modular design and central design authority allowed a complex product to be put together with less burdensome bureaucracy. Module-makers were able to concentrate on innovation in their specialist area, while the core team concentrated on innovation in the architecture of the system as a whole.

Modules could be upgraded, augmented and simplified without having to redesign the entire system. Quite soon after the S360 was introduced, IBM found that many external suppliers of modules had set up in business, specialising in peripherals and add-ons, such as applications software and disk drives. As a result, the industry as a whole grew enormously with hundreds of new firms being created around these specialisms. Eventually, IBM and other integrated computer makers lost their dominance in the industry and had to find a new role as solutions assemblers, system integrators and consultants.

Today, many more companies – such as NTT DoCoMo, the Japanese mobile operator, and Palm, the digital assistant specialist – are modelling themselves as open innovators. Modularity seems to be a potent concept for systems as complex and distributed as our health and education services. It could help us make their complexity a strength rather than a burden. What would it take to make modular and networked innovation work in the public sector?

Central design rules
Modular systems like Linux or the S360 require visible, widely shared and easily communicated design rules that set the framework for the system as a whole. These rules should be general and not too detailed but not vague. They should specify:

- the architecture of the system: what parts make up the system and the roles they play
- the interfaces that determine how the parts fit together
- the standards against which the performance of modules can be tested.

Setting out these central design rules is rarely just a technical matter. Companies like Sony, Intel and Microsoft spend huge amounts of effort persuading external developers to create products for their platform. Design rules for these systems are to some extent public goods: they allow lots of decentralised players to cooperate around common standards. Winning support for these rules and standards is as much about politics as it is about technology.

In public services the role of central departments, such as the DfES and DoH, should be to concentrate on articulating and winning support for central design rules. They should not delve too deeply into the workings of the modules that make up the system unless they are malfunctioning badly. The centre's unique role is to look after the architecture of the system as a whole.

Creating new modules

But how far can services like education and health be broken down into modules? A head teacher would argue that the quality of education at a school does not just depend on how good the individual lessons are but on the culture of the organisation as a whole. A school cannot be broken down into modules, it needs to be seen in its entirety. Modularity might make sense in complex manufactured products like cars or computers, where it is possible to specify inputs and outputs in objective, technical language – but not in a school, where quality often depends on individual judgement and initiative.

The strength of this objection needs to be acknowledged. It means there is a limit to how far modularity should be pursued. But that does not mean that services cannot adopt their own versions of modularity, which will in turn enable more open, networked innovation.

In education, for example, the most promising approach might be for each secondary school to have a set of core specialisms which help to define its ethos. These specialisms might be the modules that it concentrates on developing – music, languages, ICT or sport. The specialist school might then provide these modules to other schools in its area and in return get other specialist modules back. Schools would then increasingly become 'solutions assemblers'. Like Intel, they would need their own knowledge and ethos, to know what external modules to buy in and to transfer. But the days when each school saw itself as a vertically integrated whole, creating all aspects of education, would be gone. Instead, schools would form networks within which they could develop and trade specialist services.

Encouraging new entry is also critical. The key to the success of Fred Beck's modular design for the S360 was that it enabled a huge wave of new entries into the industry as start-ups developed to provide peripherals and applications. Within the school system, entry and exit are limited. It is difficult to close down a school and even more difficult to start one from scratch. New entry is likely to come in more subtle ways, from old schools being reconstituted through Fresh Start or the City Academies programme.

Platform innovators

If Whitehall concentrates on setting the architectural and design rules for the system, and schools are focused on innovating the basic building blocks of education, what – if any – role is there for the middle tier of local education authorities or their successors?

The answer is for the so-called middle tier in public services to become 'platform innovators'. Most hardware products these days are 'platforms' into which peripherals and accessories are plugged. When you buy a Sony computer you can also easily plug in Sony's digital camera, MP3 player or scanner. The strength of a platform is measured in part by how many of these adds-ons it can easily accommodate.[5]

Public goods are created not by the public sector acting alone, but through it forming alliances for change, which mobilise local partners, users and community groups. The best public service organisations see themselves as 'platform innovators': they create a platform of services, which then attract other players – whether local residents, community groups, the private sector or voluntary associations – to make complementary investments. The public sector cannot deliver local solutions on its own. Yet it is the only actor that can create a platform on which other players can add in their own solutions.

Epidemic change

A final ingredient of open communities of innovation is still missing: the way that new ideas spread, virally among the community, by word of mouth rather than central control.[6] An outstanding example is the history of SMS messaging over mobile phones. When SMS was created by the phone providers, they saw it as a way to fill up some wasted bandwidth. Most thought it would have only marginal use compared with voice traffic. But as consumers started using SMS, they started innovating with it and the technology spread. Out of that consumer-led innovation, bands of developers emerged creating new messaging applications. Bottom-up innovation can become systemic in scope if it becomes epidemic in scale.

Systemic innovation in the public sector needs to unlock this kind of wide-ranging change. The Conservatives might have thought they had the answer with vouchers in education, giving parents greater choice over which school to go to. But the workings of voucher schemes are invariably more costly, complex and disappointing than their advocates hope for. Labour's literacy hour, widely seen as a simple central directive, also worked by unlocking viral change, by getting thousands of teachers, kids and parents to change the way they read each day. The more that systemic change can be epidemic and bottom up, rather than engineered and top down, the better.

Open innovation in public services

How would open innovation connect McMullen and Miliband? Ros McMullen's school would be part of perhaps three secondary education 'platforms' on offer in Wigan, one run by the local education authority, another by a schools confederation and the other by a private sector provider. These platforms would consist of several schools, each of which had a specialism that they provided to the rest of the platform. One might specialise in languages, another in media, another in sport. When children signed up for secondary education, they would sign up to the platform, not just to a school. They would get access to the range of services on offer across the platform, more closely tailored to their individual aspirations. Children might move from school to school but it is more likely that the teachers would move around, bringing their specialist skills into schools that needed them.

In Whitehall, David Miliband and his officials would concentrate on setting the overall architecture and design rules within which these platforms would operate. They would help to encourage new entry, weed out under-performance and propagate new ideas by concentrating on open standards and interfaces between different parts of the system. As in all communities of innovation, change would also come in waves from the bottom up, from parents, teachers and children. Encouraging epidemic change would be as important as designing sweeping changes from on high.

This might all sound far-fetched. But go back to Fred Beck, the man in charge of developing the S360. Beck's key insight was that product innovation can only be realised when the product is made in a different way. By shifting to a modular architecture, Beck allowed the creation of a new kind of open innovation process, which in time transformed an entire industry. Had the industry not gone in that direction, it would be a great deal smaller, less diverse and less innovative. It would also be slow at learning and drowning in bureaucracy, which is where too much of the public sector remains today.

Charles Leadbeater is an author, independent adviser and Demos associate.

Notes

1   The full story of Kingsdown school is told in C Leadbeater, *The Man in the Caravan and Other Stories* (London: Improvement and Development Agency, 2003), available at www.idea.gov.uk.

2   A good account of the rise of Linux can be found in M Castells and P Himanen, *The Information Society and the Welfare State: the Finnish model* (Oxford: Oxford University Press, 2002). Also see I Tuomi, *Networks of Innovation* (Oxford: Oxford University Press, 2002).

3   See H Chesbrough, *Open Innovation* (Boston, Mass.: Harvard Business School

Press, 2003) and B Nooteboom, *Learning and Innovation in Organisations and Economies* (Oxford: Oxford University Press, 2000).

4   For detailed studies of the System 360 and the rise of modular approach to innovation see C Baldwin and K Clark, *Design Rules: the power of modularity* (Boston, Mass.: MIT Press, 2000) and R Garud, A Kumaraswamy and R Langlois (eds) *Managing in the Modular Age: architectures, networks and organisations* (Oxford: Blackwell, 2003).

5   For a useful description of platform innovation see A Gawer and M Cusumano, *Platform Leadership* (Boston, Mass.: Harvard Business School Press, 2003).

6   Among several accounts of epidemic and vital change see M Gladwell *The Tipping Point* (London: Abacus, 2002) and S Godin, *The Idea Virus* (New York: Simon & Schuster, 2002).

3. Thinking out of the machine

Jake Chapman

There is a growing recognition that a new approach is needed to radically improve the state of public service delivery in the UK. In this essay I argue that the core change required to develop and implement effective policies is in the mental models that are used to think about public services and the organisations involved in their delivery. For at least the last 50 years, ways of thinking have been based on scientific management and the use of mechanistic metaphors. It is the implicit and outdated assumptions embedded within these ways of thinking that are undermining the good intentions of politicians and policy-makers today. Changing these assumptions is a significant challenge. Yet, once accomplished, change opens the way for resolving many of the conflicts that currently confuse and obstruct the agenda for modernising and improving public services.

The dominance of scientific management and mechanistic thinking in the ways that policy-makers – civil servants and politicians – think about policy becomes obvious in any conversation on the topic. Phrases such as 'the machinery of government', 'driving through change', 'stepping up a gear' and 'policy levers' are all based on images of machines. Scientific management, which arose in the era when production lines were being developed, encourages its users to think of organisations in terms of such mechanical images. As Geoff Mulgan has pointed out,

*The ubiquity of the machine metaphor was the legacy that the
military bequeathed to governments and then to
manufacturing . . . Well-oiled, efficient and measurable, the
ideal machine had a clear purpose or function which it carried
out perfectly. Everything . . . consisting of cogs and wheels,
instructions and commands, with a boss or government at the
top, pulling the requisite levers and engineering the desired
effects.*[1]

However, as he also points out, 'the environment for machine-like
things has gone into decline' – and it is this that causes this mode of
thinking to undermine good intentions.

There are many implicit assumptions associated with mechanistic
thinking and scientific management, but the two that are at the root
of so many current difficulties are:

O the assumption of control: that organisations can be
  controlled in the way that machines can be controlled, to
  behave differently and produce different outputs
O the presumption that the organisations involved in
  'delivery' behave in a predictable fashion so that the effects
  of interventions and policies can be predicted.

A moment's reflection will demonstrate that challenging or rejecting
these assumptions undermines a great deal about current policy
thinking. If the organisations responsible for delivering public
services cannot be controlled then what can be done? If their
behaviour cannot be predicted then how can any sort of policy be
devised? There are cogent answers to these questions, but before they
can be realised it is essential to grasp the nettle and recognise the
degree to which control and predictability are myths.

The key reasons why organisations cannot be controlled or
predicted in a mechanical way can be illustrated by a metaphor first
developed by Richard Dawkins involving throwing things.[2] Newton's

laws of motion and gravity enable us to predict with a great deal of precision the force and inclination required to throw a rock (or weapon) to arrive at a predetermined destination (the target). However, this approach fails utterly if the object being thrown is a bird. The bird remains governed by Newton's laws – it does not defy the laws of physics – but there is something about its internal organisation that causes it to respond differently from the way an inanimate object would respond.

Public services as complex adaptive systems

This bird–rock metaphor illustrates the significance of internal organisation in what are known as complex adaptive systems. The concept of a complex adaptive system is central to understanding why mechanistic thinking is obstructive in policy, so let me explain it in some detail.

By referring to something as a system I am attributing characteristics to the whole entity that cannot be accounted for by properties of the component parts; in some sense the whole is greater than the sum of the parts. Another way of expressing this is to say that, when regarded as a whole, properties emerge that are not present in the individual parts. An obvious example is the emergent property of vision that arises from a combination of cells associated with the eye and the brain; the property of vision is not within any of the components and only emerges when the components interact in a certain organised fashion. Complexity and adaptation are two emergent properties of many systems.

Complexity has become something of a fashionable term, though it is rarely used with any degree of precision. Being complex is not the same as being complicated. Both involve the idea of lots of components interacting together. But the key difference is that something that is complicated may still be predictable whereas a central part of what is meant by complexity is being unpredictable. In human systems the source of complexity and unpredictability is the interaction of autonomous agents. Greater complexity and lower predictability stem from a greater number of agents, greater autonomy of agents and/or more interactions and exchange of messages. Economic markets are a paradigmatic example of a complex human system.

A system is said to be adaptive when it has some way of coordinating its behaviour or responses in such a way as to protect some core structure or values. In the biological world adaptation occurs in response to environmental changes and is unpredictable in detail. Organisations can be regarded as adaptive systems and will behave in ways that resist attempts to make them change; this is a sign of their resilience. However, for those wishing to enforce a change this adaptive potential will be experienced as resistance. One of the characteristics of adaptive responses is that they are generally non-linear. By this I mean that small changes can sometimes lead to a very large change within the system whereas on other occasions quite large changes lead to no change in the system. There is not a linear relationship between the input or stimulus for change and the output or change in system configuration. This is another source of unpredictability in such systems.

So the core argument I am making is that organisations, in particular those engaged in the provision of public services, have more in common with complex adaptive systems than with machines. As such they cannot be controlled or predicted, in much the same way that throwing a bird does not lead to the same degree of control or predictability as throwing a rock. Confronted with this obvious truth, control freaks have suggested that one way to get the bird to the 'target' is to tie a rock to it so that it cannot use its wings, which would certainly make it behave more like a rock. But it also destroys the key attributes of the bird. Elsewhere I have pointed out that this is much the same as managing a complex organisation as if it were a machine – with the same destructive results.[3] I have also explained and illustrated that adopting a mechanistic approach leads to ever-increasing unintended consequences, a reduction in system capacity and the alienation of professional and other front-line staff.

But to what degree is it valid to regard organisations as complex adaptive systems? If mechanistic thinking and scientific management worked in the past what has changed? There are two key ingredients in human affairs that are involved here. The first is an increase in individual autonomy and the second is the phenomenal increase in the number of communications technologies over the last century. The increase in autonomy arises as a result of the emphasis on individualism, the unwillingness to accept authority unquestioningly and the loss of agreed interpretations because of different cultures and perspectives. Communications technologies, starting with telephone and radio and ending with mobile phones and the internet, have dramatically reduced the costs and barriers to communication and exchange of information. Together these have increased the autonomy and interaction of the agents that make up organisations and have now reached a threshold that requires a new way of thinking.

The value of a systems approach

The fact that organisations may behave more like complex adaptive systems than machines does not mean that they cannot be managed or influenced, but it requires a different approach based on systems thinking. There are three broad strategies available.

The bird–rock metaphor can be used to illustrate the first option. Rather than trying to force the bird to a given point a better strategy would be to place a bird table with the bird's favourite food at the desired destination. This is providing an attractor for the system. In the case of organisations and humans, attractors are the things that humans want to do, things that fulfil some core purpose or function, things that provide meaning and fulfilment. Attractors are not hard to find: teachers love teaching, doctors love to heal people and housing officers love putting people in decent accommodation that suits their requirements. The key to the successful use of attractors is to cease using coercive management approaches since these demotivate the people whose enthusiasm and commitment are required for strategy based on attractors to be successful.

The second approach is to make use of a management style based on the concept of a learning organisation.[4] A key feature of this style is that the approach to the organisation is that of learning what works, rather than presuming that this can be known or deduced from analysis. In order to be effective this approach must be:

O   tolerant of failure and willing to learn from successes and failures
O   based on quantitative and qualitative feedback on outcomes
O   based on cooperation with service delivery staff and other stakeholders in the design, evaluation and subsequent modification of improvements.

The civil service culture makes learning difficult, particularly by the practices of generalism, delegating upwards, time pressures, inward focus and mechanistic thinking (as manifest in performance management and targets). But the greatest single obstacle to adopting a learning approach is the belief, by individuals or groups, that they already know the right thing to do. Adopting a learning posture means acknowledging, to oneself and to others, that no one yet knows the best way to intervene in the complex system being managed.

The third strategy is for the manager to foster innovation and variety and then to select from the range of outcomes those that are consistent with the required direction of change. This is an evolutionary approach and is extremely useful when carrying out pilot trials where there is very little prior evidence of what works.

One thing that all these strategies have in common is that they give up the notion that it is possible to control the complex system. This is easy in theory, but much harder in practice. Managers at all levels will have a fear of acknowledging that the system they are managing is outside their control – they are likely to experience this as some sort of failing on their part. It is essential that this fear of loss of control is acknowledged and managed explicitly – otherwise the manager will try to reassert control – either by using more scientific manage-ment or by trying to subvert the above approaches into control strategies.

It should be emphasised that without a shift in thinking it is unlikely that any of these systemic management strategies will lead to significant improvement. Shifting attitudes and modes of thinking is not easy, especially when working in an environment where most other agencies and individuals are thinking mechanically and assuming you still share their perspective. What is required is a learning process at all levels: the personal, the group and the organisational.

The importance of experiential learning

It is important to distinguish between two different types of learning, both of which are essential in establishing a learning organisation. The first, referred to as skills learning, is acquired through a process of training or education or assimilation. This type of learning includes developing skills in project management, negotiation, budget control, analysis of data and so on.

The second type of learning can be referred to as systemic learning or learning from experience. This type of learning is not dispensed by teachers or training agencies but is undertaken by individuals and groups as part of their regular work activity. It requires the individual or group to reflect consciously on the effects or impact of their recent activities or interventions and to use the results of that reflection to inform their future actions and strategies. This type of systemic learning is also known as the learning cycle. The key feature is that the individual or group reflects on their experience of their actions and uses the results of that reflection to influence future actions.

The aim of these learning processes is not to impose some sort of thought control, but to become aware of the mode of thinking being employed and to reflect on its assumptions, appropriateness and prescriptions. This awareness will foster reflection on experience and enable managers to develop their own approach to using the new way of thinking. A simple but effective way to start becoming aware of how one is thinking about a situation is to ask the following questions each time one experiences difficulties or conflicts:

O   How would my perspective change if I regarded this
     organisation (agency or department) as a complex
     system?
O   What approach would I adopt if I accepted that this
     system could not be controlled or predicted?
O   What other perspectives are there on this issue and how
     can I understand them?
O   How can I learn what is most effective here? How would I
     know?
O   What relationships are essential in moving forward and
     how can I nurture them?

Conclusion

The argument on which this essay is based is that the world in which
government operates has changed to such a degree that the
established ways of thinking, generating policies and managing public
services no longer work. The key changes that invalidate current
policy and management approaches are the increasing autonomy of
individuals and the widespread adoption of communications
technologies. These changes nullify the presumptions of control and
predictability embedded within the current approach to improving
public services and mean that policies generate more unintended
consequences than successful outcomes. To some degree it is this
ineffectiveness of government that contributes to political apathy and
distrust.

Before more effective forms of policy-making, governance and
management of public services can emerge it is essential that the
presumptions of control and predictability, buried in the established
ways of thinking, are abandoned. If new styles of policy and
management are developed without giving up the notions of control
and predictability then the new styles will fail as surely as the old.
Giving up control and prediction requires courage, a willingness to be
aware of how one thinks and a desire to find out what works by a
process of exploration and reflection.

Once the myth of control is abandoned then the debate about

granting autonomy to hospitals is transformed – simply because control is recognised as not being an option. If the myth of predictability is abandoned then targets cease to have such a grip on political and media attention – simply because it is not possible for anyone to predict outcomes in these complex situations. With predictability and control abandoned it becomes clear that policies devised centrally on the basis of rational analysis are inappropriate – because they are based on the presumption that it is possible to know in advance how a complex system will behave. It is also the case that if control, predictability and centralised policies are recognised by government as inappropriate then professionals and delivery staff in the public services would breathe a sigh of relief and engage with enthusiasm in agendas of improvement and reform.

For some, the prescription advocated here may appear too idealistic, and for others giving up control and predictability may appear too frightening. What is certain is that until mechanistic modes of thinking are given up, nothing much will change. Indeed, the current government will progressively lose credibility as its attempts at reform and improvement continue to stall. But if control and predictability are given up, new possibilities will emerge and we can look forward to a brighter future for our public services.

Jake Chapman is a systems expert and author of the Demos pamphlet, System Failure: why governments must learn to think differently.

Notes

1   G Mulgan, *Connexity: responsibility, freedom, business and power in the new century* (London: Vintage Books, 1997).
2   As described in P Plsek, 'Why won't the NHS do as it's told?', paper to NHS conference, July 2001.
3   J Chapman, *System Failure: why governments must learn to think differently* (London: Demos, 2002).
4   See for example P Senge, *The Fifth Discipline: the art and practice of the learning organisation* (London: Random House, 1990).

4. Leadership, reform and learning in public services

Bob Fryer

Intellectual fads and fashions always worry me, especially where they concern the world of work. They often begin, quite promisingly, with some scholar or senior practitioner opening up a new perspective on a traditional field of enquiry or action with their radical conceptual insights, challenging empirical findings or exemplary professional experience. Their initiative then excites further debate, theoretical refinement and, too often, linguistic elaboration. Soon, what began as a serious-minded contribution to thinking and practice emerges as the latest and most urgent answer to organisational strategy, effectiveness, growth, competitiveness and change. Before long, attractive texts with engaging or quirky titles on the subject can be picked up on every railway and airport bookstall. Frequently, initial serious-mindedness and balanced analysis give way to simplistic nostrum, heroic example and knee-jerk, 'cook-book' recipes for action. Instant interventions of a peculiar kind are promised just around the corner – frequently to be gleaned in the longueurs of a flight or train journey – the soft porn of organisational life at the top.

So it is with the three aspects of organisational and public life addressed in this paper – leadership, reform and learning – which are increasingly linked together in policy and practice. The briefest of internet or library searches will deliver thousands of references to leadership, most of them penned in the last ten years. Amazon UK alone lists more than 13,000 book titles available on the subject. You can more or less take your pick. Leadership 'gurus' abound, and their international lifestyles attest to their appeal and to their own sharp business acumen in successfully selling the business of business. (Expensive) leadership development programmes abound in the world's best business schools, in leading companies and, increasingly, in public sector organisations such as the civil service, health and local government. Even universities are now sending potential future vice chancellors on leadership programmes. Being selected to join such a programme confirms either membership of a key organisational elite or early promise of future preference. If you want to get to the top, it seems that participation in a top-flight leadership programme must now figure in your curriculum vitae. The only trouble is, in this embarrassment of choice, exactly how do you know whether or not you have selected the right text, the best programme or the most useful master class? It all seems to be rather context free.

Similarly, learning, in all of its various forms and manifestations, now figures in every CEO or senior politician's repertoire of key priorities for success. So, the focus may be on 'education, education, education', or on one of 57 varieties of the 'learning organisation', on the discovery of and systematic investment in 'talent', on learning and creativity or on the pressing demands of the development of skills. There are signs too of a growing recognition that many of those people thought likely to gain most from investment in their learning at work receive far too few opportunities, get much too little managerial support and have insufficient organisational resources allocated to their cause. But, even where this is not the case, many such staff still understandably question why they should be expected to endure the challenges and excitements of learning, only to return to familiar and continuing occupational and career restrictions with few real opportunities to deploy their new-found capabilities.

While almost nobody now will gainsay the potentially vital contribution that learning can make to individual and organisational achievement, to date few reliable metrics exist to provide robust evidence for such confident claims. Moreover, there is still insufficient understanding of the profound transformations in work organisation and responsibility needed to complement learning, as well as those improvements in service delivery that might be expected to follow from its systematic impact. And we all know that learning is an expensive, time-consuming and often (rightly) subversive business. So exactly what kind of learning, for which people, with what objectives and delivered in what modes and forms should be preferred?

Finally, politicians, journalists, scholars and trades unionists are now much exercised by what is widely seen as the related challenge of so-called 'modernising' of the public services, now that the crude touchstones of privatisation – contracting out and hiving off – have all been revealed as deeply flawed. Great stress is being given to the urgency of reform, with a focus on the need for much greater and more fleet-footed responsiveness to the desires, interests and preferences of service users, as against the alleged prevalence of widespread risk-aversion, producer-driven practices and ingrained professional 'tribalism' of the staff involved.

Eschewing the quick fix

But no quick fix, instant solutions are readily to hand. Only the ideologically blinkered would now argue that simply imposing vulgar 'marketisation' on the public services will secure the range and scale of transformation required without simultaneously squandering the palpable commitment, dedication and professionalism of the workforce on which successful service delivery and reform ultimately depend. After all, there is precious little hard evidence that the pressure of markets alone constitutes a sufficient driver of the change now being asked of the public services, although there is still much to emulate in the best functioning markets, which constantly strive for the sovereignty of service users. We should also question the equally simple notion that approaches that appear to have worked reasonably well in the private sector can, with only modest adjustment and adaptation, be easily applied in the very different sphere of public service. Above all, failure to recognise the distinctive, deep values-based nature of public services and of their workforces will confound any such crude misapplication. This point is demonstrated by the innovative, practice-based and very challenging work on 'public value' being pioneered, among others, by Professor Mark Moore of the Kennedy School at Harvard University.[1]

Values and value

So, what is there to be said that is new, that avoids the evident pitfalls of following the latest fashion or championing the most recent (and recently published) style guide? First, we need to recognise that neither the government's acknowledgment of the key role played by values in public services design and delivery, nor the genuine commitment to public services values among many staff, guarantees effective alignment between government commitment, the practices of service providers and the desires and preferences of the public. There is much to be done here, not least in opening up for more thorough and informed debate the putative and powerful core public service values of, for example, fairness, equity and responsiveness.

These values cannot be taken for granted, nor can their everyday manifestation be assumed to occur in the current organisation of public services or in the best (let alone routine) professional behaviour of staff. Second, understanding, developing and responding to the explicit, diverse and changing expectations of a public engaged as full citizens and not merely as customers will make huge demands on public institutions, not least in their functions as the 'educators of desire'. Third, if this process is properly engaged, we should also expect it to have radical implications for the education, qualification and professional practice of staff at all levels, including those in positions of leadership, and for the operations and management of public service organisations. Fourth, such a profound transformation can only occur if we institute a much richer, more active and better informed conception of citizenship than our currently rather formal, limited and impoverished model represents. Finally, a more critical, involved, educated and challenging citizenry will not be willing to allow either politicians or service provider leaders to claim an intuitive or privileged grasp of public wants and dissatisfactions. Nor will these previously dominant groups be free, paternalistically, to substitute their well-intentioned, but often arbitrary, priorities for the more complex, diffuse, contradictory and shifting needs of service users, their loved ones and the public at large.

Citizenship, learning and service enhancement

So here is a multiple and complex role for learning that extends way beyond the admittedly vital and still inadequately delivered functions of developing and enhancing staff skills, improving managerial effectiveness, securing more efficient use of resources and improving user experience in the public services. It means enlisting public service leadership and learning in the difficult process of drawing citizens into the very definition, design, delivery and review of public services. It means shifting the principal organisational form for public services towards one that resembles much more a network of knowledge, information, service design and delivery than the typically self-sufficient, tightly structured and imperatively coordinated institutions that have hitherto dominated.[2] Radical shifts such as these will constitute some of the grounds on which to base a richer and more demanding sense of trust in the public services, and their continuing legitimate claim on public resources.

Creating and sustaining such relationships between individuals, communities and citizens' services will threaten many vested interests, inside and outside the public sector. These include the views and behaviour of politicians, the private business sector, the media as well as the more obvious bailiwicks of public service professions, trades unions and managers. The very idea that current variations in the quality, shape and calibre of public service provision can be attributed principally to the staff working in the services is naïve, incomplete and pernicious. Just think for a moment of the impact of private pharmaceutical companies on healthcare provision or of the manufacturers of food and drink on public health. All can, and should, be challenged by an unfolding notion of 'public value' and an increasingly learning and actively involved citizenry.

The role of leadership in such circumstances will be to orchestrate and facilitate the educated engagement of all parties and to mobilise resources and people in delivering the changes and priorities in public service provision identified through such processes as effective outcomes. This kind of process requires leaders to put in place sustainable and innovative 'knowledge life cycles' in networked organisations.[3]

This poses the challenge for leaders to engineer open systems and service cultures that emphasise the combination of new knowledge production with its full integration into all organisational processes. That means successfully securing commitment to an innovative approach to knowledge and information throughout the whole organisation, and across its boundaries. It also means stimulating self-organising energy in the production, diffusion and application of new knowledge aimed at transforming service delivery. The burning question for public service leaders in this will be how to integrate such a radical approach to service improvement into what are, traditionally, highly regulated, deeply hierarchical, professionally differentiated, rule-driven, rigidly boundaried, politically controlled and mostly 'closed' public service organisations. Such integration simply cannot be achieved without a radical shake-up of work processes, relationships and responsibilities, as well as of learning. Will politicians reconcile themselves to circumstances where setting strategic priorities is no longer their exclusive role?

Transforming learning

There are even more serious contradictions, paradoxes and challenges here for those engaged in the provision and development of such learning. What content should be on offer? How best can learners be engaged and supported? How can fair access to learning opportunities and facilities be secured? What mechanisms can be deployed to enable learners to fit learning into their own lives, priorities and preferred ways of learning? What part will be afforded in this to informal learning and the tacit knowledge and practice of different communities and their own traditions of literacy and understanding, so often driven out and undermined by conventional education? And, who should decide all of this?

These questions need to be set against a background where, too often in this country, education has not only been the very site manifesting inequalities of learning opportunity and attainment but, more worrying still, a principal means of distributing and reinforcing inequity and the restriction of imagination, ambition and achievement. If learning is to play a key part in reform, who will reform the (potential) reformers? Of course, there is a role here for innovative educational leaders, defending and advancing the case for giving priority to the development of well-informed, critical thinking, curious and open-minded citizens in the cause of public service reform. But that of itself will not be enough. Learning itself will need to be the focus of transformation, as well as serving to support the advancement of a richer and more multifaceted notion of public value.

A reformed and reforming learning will need to examine critically its own ways and means. Naturally, learning in its many varied manifestations will still need to benefit to a very considerable extent from the sorts of specialisms, concentration of resources, facilities, expertise and institutional regularity that we associate with schools, colleges, universities, timetables, courses and qualifications. But, more and more, that will not be enough. As Michael Barber once insightfully predicted, we shall increasingly also need to find learning in the most surprising and unlikely places if the kind of relationship between public services and engaged citizenship advocated here is to stand any chance of developing.[4]

And that will also mean not only availing ourselves of the best of the new information and communications, but also ensuring that democratic and equitable access to such resources are guaranteed in or by the public sphere. Evidence to date suggests a widening information and technology divide in our society that already threatens the universal use and value of e-learning and the development of a democratic e-citizenship. Not even the promised advent of popular digital broadcasting will be enough to inscribe these exciting prospects for learning into the everyday life chances of all citizens, of every social background and status.

Learning to navigate a risk society

This kind of approach to leadership and service reform, shaped more energetically and imaginatively by learning citizens, will have to succeed in a world whose shape is becoming more indeterminate for public and services alike. That world is best captured, in my view, by the emerging notion of the 'risk society' first outlined by Ulrich Beck and others just over a decade ago.[5] According to Beck, people and organisations in the twenty-first century will increasingly require the capacity and confidence to navigate an environment characterised by ambiguity, uncertainty, unpredictability and unreliability. The decline of certainty in scientific knowledge and traditional institutional expertise leads towards an era of contested knowledge, information overload, fears about sustainability and deepening social divisions. Increasingly the task is to deal effectively with 'fuzzy' boundaries (as, for example, between service providers and service users) and to operate in a world where there are no pre-existing rules to guide conduct. This is a world in which individuals, communities and whole societies must be able to engage with change, not as its mere victims, but as its active and informed authors. In such a world the reforming public services and a more active citizenry should be served by a richer, more accessible and more challenging array of learning opportunities, forms, modes and styles. Engaging successfully with this startling and unprecedented combination of changes, as facilitator and respondent, constitutes the single biggest challenge to public leadership in our time.

Professor Bob Fryer is chief executive of the NHSU.

Notes

1   MH Moore, *Creating Public Value: strategic management in government* (Cambridge, Mass.: Harvard University Press, 1995).
2   C Leadbeater, *Living on Thin Air: the new economy* (London: Viking, 1999).

3   MW McElroy, *The New Knowledge Management: complexity, learning and sustainable innovation* (Oxford: Butterworth-Heinemann, 2002).

4   M Barber, *The Learning Game: arguments for an educational revolution* (London: Victor Gollancz, 1996).

5   U Beck, *Risk Society: towards a new modernity* (London: Sage, 1992).

5. Adaptive work

Ronald A. Heifetz

Our language fails us in many aspects of our lives, entrapping us in a set of cultural assumptions like cattle herded by fences into a corral. Gender pronouns, for example, corral us into teaching children that God is a he, distancing girls and women every day from the experience of the divine in themselves.

Our language fails us, too, when we discuss, analyse and practise leadership. We commonly talk about 'leaders' in organisations or politics when we actually mean people in positions of managerial or political authority. Although we have confounded leadership with authority in nearly every journalistic and scholarly article written on 'leadership' during the last one hundred years, we know intuitively that these two phenomena are distinct when we complain all too frequently in politics and business that 'the leadership isn't exercising any leadership', by which we actually mean to say that 'people in authority aren't exercising any leadership'. Whether people with formal, charismatic or otherwise informal authority actually practise leadership on any given issue at any moment in time ought to remain a separate question answered with wholly different criteria from those used to define a relationship of formal or informal authority. As we know, all too many people are skilled at gaining authority, and thus a following, but do not then lead.

Moreover, we assume a logical connection between the words 'leader and follower', as if this dyad were an absolute and inherently logical structure. It is not. The most interesting leadership operates without anyone experiencing anything remotely similar to the experience of 'following'. Indeed, most leadership mobilises those who are opposed or who sit on the fence, in addition to allies and friends. Allies and friends come relatively cheap; it's the people in opposition who have the most to lose in any significant process of change. When mobilised, allies and friends become not followers but active participants – employees or citizens who themselves often lead in turn by taking responsibility for tacking tough challenges, often beyond expectations and often beyond their authority. They become partners. And when mobilised, opposition and fence-sitters become engaged with the issues, provoked to work through the problems of loss, loyalty and competence embedded in the change they are challenged to make. Indeed, they may continue to fight, providing an ongoing source of diverse views necessary for the adaptive success of the business or community. Far from becoming 'aligned' and far from any experience of 'following', they are mobilised by leadership to wrestle with new complexities that demand tough trade-offs in their ways of working or living. Of course, in time they may begin to trust, admire and appreciate the person or group that is leading, and thereby confer informal authority on them, but they would not generally experience the emergence of that appreciation or trust by the phrase: 'I've become a follower.'

This puts the struggle to reform public services to produce radically better social outcomes for citizens in an important new light. It may mean that policies for 'leadership' must go beyond conferring extra authority or heaping greater expectation on those who occupy positions of public authority. It places a premium instead on mobilising a more responsible citizenship, which includes the 'embracing' of people actively opposed to the direction and manifestations of change. Perhaps most important, it means that public deliberation and public debate about the normative value of the goals towards which leadership energy is directed take on crucial importance.

If leadership is different from the capacity to gain formal or informal authority, and therefore different from the ability to gain a 'following' – attracting influence and accruing power – what can anchor our understanding of it?

Leadership takes place in the context of problems and challenges. Indeed, it makes little sense to describe leadership when everything and everyone in an organisation is humming along just fine, even when processes of influence and authority will be virtually ubiquitous in coordinating routine activity. Leadership becomes necessary to businesses and communities when people have to change their ways rather than continue to operate according to current structures, procedures and processes. Beyond technical problems, for which authoritative and managerial expertise will suffice, adaptive challenges demand leadership that can engage people in facing challenging realities and then changing at least some of their priorities, attitudes and behaviour in order to thrive in a changing world.

Mobilising people to meet adaptive challenges, then, is at the heart of leadership practice. In the short term, leadership is an activity that mobilises people to meet an immediate challenge. In the medium and long term, leadership generates new cultural norms that enable people to meet an ongoing stream of adaptive challenges in a world that will likely pose an ongoing set of adaptive realities and pressures. Thus, with a longer view, leadership develops an organisation or community's adaptive capacity or adaptability. This investment in adaptability should be part of the social vision offered by political leadership, as well as part of the organisational strategies that constitute the reform process. In this short article, we suggest seven different ways to describe and understand adaptive work.

The adaptive challenge

First, an adaptive challenge is a problem situation for which solutions lie outside the current way of operating. We can distinguish technical problems, which are amenable to current expertise, from adaptive challenges, which are not. Although every problem can be understood as a gap between aspirations and reality, technical problems present a gap between aspirations and reality that can be closed through applying existing know-how. For example, a patient comes to his doctor with an infection, and the doctor uses her knowledge to diagnose the illness and prescribe a cure.

In contrast, an adaptive challenge is created by a gap between a desired state and reality that cannot be closed using existing approaches alone. Progress in the situation requires more than the application of current expertise, authoritative decision-making, standard operating procedures or culturally informed behaviours. For example, a patient with heart disease may need to change his way of life: diet, exercise, smoking and the imbalances that cause unhealthy stress. To make those changes, the patient will have to take responsibility for his health and learn his way to a new set of priorities and habits.

This distinction is summarised in Figure 1.

Figure 1 Technical and adaptive work[1]

Kind of work	Problem definition	Solutions and implementation	Primary locus of responsibility for the work
Technical	Clear	Clear	Authority
Technical & adaptive	Clear	Requires learning	Authority stakeholder
Adaptive	Requires learning	Requires learning	Stakeholder >authority

The demand for learning

Second, adaptive challenges demand learning. An adaptive challenge exists when the people themselves are the problem and when progress requires a retooling, in a sense, of their own ways of thinking and operating. The gap between aspirations and reality closes when they learn new ways. Thus, a consulting firm may offer a brilliant diagnostic analysis and set of recommendations, but nothing will be solved until that analysis and those recommendations are lived in the new way that people operate. Until then, the consultant has no solutions, only proposals.

Shift responsibility to the stakeholders

Third, adaptive challenges require a shift in responsibility from the shoulders of the authority figures and the authority structure to the stakeholders themselves. In contrast to expert problem-solving, adaptive work requires a different form of deliberation and a different way of taking responsibility. In doing adaptive work, responsibility needs to be felt in a far more widespread fashion. At best, an organisation would have its members know that there are many technical problems for which looking to authority for answers is appropriate and efficient, but that for the adaptive set of challenges looking to authority for answers becomes self-defeating. When people make the classic error of treating adaptive challenges as if they were technical, they wait for the person in authority to know what to do.[2] He or she then makes a best guess – probably just a guess – while the many sit back and wait to see whether the guess pans out. And frequently enough, when it does not, people get rid of that executive and go find another one, all the while operating under the illusion that 'if only we had the right "leader", our problems would be solved'. Progress is impeded by inappropriate dependency, and thus a major task of leadership is the development of responsibility-taking by stakeholders themselves.

Distinguish between the essential and the expendable

Fourth, an adaptive challenge requires people to distinguish between what is precious and essential and what is expendable within their culture. In cultural adaptation, the job is to take the best from history, leave behind that which is no longer serviceable, and through innovation learn ways to thrive in the new environment.

Therefore, adaptive work is inherently conservative as well as progressive. The point of innovation is to conserve what is best from history as the community moves into the future. As in biology, a successful adaptation takes the best from its past set of competencies and loses the DNA that is no longer useful. Thus, unlike many current conceptions of culturally 'transforming' processes, many of which are ahistorical – as if one begins all anew – adaptive work, profound as it may be in terms of change, must honour ancestry and history at the same time that it challenges them.

Adaptive work generates resistance in people because adaptation requires us to let go of certain elements of our past ways of working or living, which means to experience loss – loss of competence, loss of reporting relationships, loss of jobs, loss of traditions or loss of loyalty to the people who taught us the lessons of our heritage. Thus, an adaptive challenge generates a situation that forces us to make tough trade-offs. The source of resistance that people have to change is not resistance to change *per se*; it is resistance to loss. People love change when they know it is beneficial. Nobody gives the lottery ticket back when they win. Leadership must contend, then, with the various forms of feared and real losses that accompany adaptive work.[3]

Anchored to the tasks of mobilising people to thrive in new and challenging contexts, leadership is not simply about change; more profoundly leadership is about identifying that which is worth conserving. It is the conserving of the precious dimensions of our past that make the pains of change worth sustaining.

Experiment

Fifth, adaptive work demands experimentation. In biology, the adaptability of a species depends on the multiplicity of experiments that are being run constantly within its gene pool, increasing the odds that in that distributed intelligence some diverse members of the species will have the means to succeed in a new context. Similarly, in cultural adaptation, an organisation or community needs to be running multiple experiments and learning fast from these experiments in order to see 'which horses to ride into the future'.

Appropriate and efficient problem-solving depends on

authoritative experts for knowledge and decisive action. In contrast, dealing with adaptive challenges requires a comfort with not knowing where to go or how to move next. In mobilising adaptive work from an authority position, leadership takes the form of protecting elements of deviance and creativity in the organisation in spite of the inefficiencies associated with those elements. If creative or outspoken people generate conflict, then so be it. Conflict becomes an engine of innovation, rather than solely a source of dangerous inefficiency. Managing the dynamic tension between creativity and efficiency becomes an ongoing part of leadership practice for which there exists no equilibrium point at which this tension disappears. Leadership becomes an improvisation, however frustrating it may be not to know the answers.

The time frame of adaptive work

Sixth, the time frame of adaptive work is markedly different from that of technical work. It takes time for people to learn new ways – to sift through what is precious from what is expendable, and to innovate in ways that enable people to carry forward into the future that which they continue to hold precious from the past. Moses took 40 years to bring the children of Israel to the Promised Land, not because it was such a long walk from Egypt, but because it took that much time for the people to leave behind the dependent mentality of slavery and generate the capacity for self-government guided by faith in something ineffable. Figure 2 depicts this difference in time frame.

Because it is so difficult for people to sustain prolonged periods of disturbance and uncertainty, human beings naturally engage in a variety of efforts to restore equilibrium as quickly as possible, even if it means avoiding adaptive work and begging the tough issues. Most forms of adaptive failure are a product of our difficulty in containing prolonged periods of experimentation, and the difficult conversations that accompany them.

Work avoidance is simply the natural effort to restore a more familiar order, to restore equilibrium. Although many different forms of work avoidance operate across cultures and peoples, it appears that

Figure 2 Technical problem or adaptive challenge?

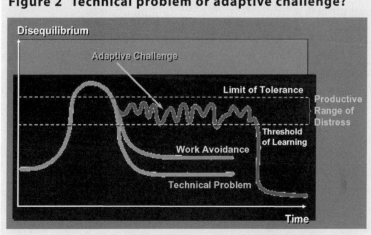

there are two common pathways: the displacement of responsibility and the diversion of attention. Both pathways work terribly well in the short term, even if they leave people more exposed and vulnerable in the medium and long term. Some common forms of displacing responsibility include scapegoating, blaming the persistence of problems on authority, externalising the enemy or killing the messenger. Diverting attention can take the form of fake remedies, like the Golden Calf; an effort to define problems to fit one's competence; repeated structural adjustments; the faulty use of consultants, committees and task forces; sterile conflicts and proxy fights ('let's watch the gladiator fight!'); or outright denial.

Adaptive work is a normative concept

Finally, adaptive work is a normative concept. The concept of adaptation arises from scientific efforts to understand biological evolution.[4] Applied to the change of cultures and societies, the concept becomes a useful, if inexact, metaphor.[5] For example, species evolve whereas cultures learn. Evolution is generally understood by scientists as a matter of chance, whereas societies will often consciously deliberate, plan and intentionally experiment. Close to our normative concern, biological evolution conforms to laws of survival. Societies, on the other hand, generate purposes beyond survival. The concept of adaptation applied to culture raises the question: adapt to what, for what purpose?

In biology, the 'objective function' of adaptive work is straightforward: to thrive in new environments. Survival of the self and of one's gene-carrying kin defines the direction in which animals adapt. A situation becomes an adaptive challenge because it threatens the capacity of a species to pass on its genetic heritage. Thus, when a species multiplies its own kind and succeeds in passing on its genes, it is said to be 'thriving' in its environment.

Thriving is more than coping. There is nothing trivial in biology about adaptation. Some adaptive leaps transform the capacity of a species by sparking an ongoing and profound process of adaptive change that leads to a vastly expanded range of living.

In human societies, 'thriving' takes on a host of values not restricted to survival of one's own kind. At times, human beings will even trade off their own survival for values like liberty, justice and faith. Thus, adaptive work in cultures involves the clarification of values and the assessment of realities that challenge the realisation of those values.

Because most organisations and communities honour a mix of values, the competition within this mix largely explains why adaptive work so often involves conflict. People with competing values engage one another as they confront a shared situation from their own points of view. At its extreme, and in the absence of better methods of social change, the conflict over values can be violent. The American Civil War changed the meaning of union and individual freedom. In 1857, ensuring domestic tranquillity meant returning escaped slaves to their owners; in 1957, it meant using federal troops to integrate Central High School in Little Rock.

Some realities threaten not only a set of values beyond survival, but also the very existence of a society if these realities are not discovered and met early on by the value-clarifying and reality-testing functions of that society. In the view of many environmentalists, for example, our focus on the production of wealth rather than on coexistence with nature has led us to neglect fragile factors in our ecosystem. These factors may become relevant to us when finally they begin to challenge our central values of health and survival, but by then we may have paid a high price in damage already done, and the costs of and odds against adaptive adjustment may have increased enormously.[6]

Conclusion

Adaptive work, then, requires us to deliberate on the values by which we seek to thrive, and demands diagnostic enquiry into the realities we face that threaten the realisation of those values. Beyond legitimising a convenient set of assumptions about reality, beyond denying or avoiding the internal contradictions in some of the values we hold precious, and beyond coping, adaptive work involves proactively seeking to clarify aspirations or develop new ones, and then involves the very hard work of innovation, experimentation and cultural change to realise a closer approximation of those aspirations by which we would define 'thriving'.

This constitutes a challenge for our systems of democracy, as well as those of governance and public service delivery. The forms of thriving that public services should support do not remain static. The ways in which they can or should be supported must be tested by public deliberation and by organisational experimentation. Yet citizens are generally ill-prepared for legislation or policy framed as 'experimentation'. All too often citizens crave solutions, not trial efforts or pilot projects, and therefore put a great deal of pressure on politicians and public servants to overstate the promise of new policies and programmatic instruments. When those promises then fall short, trust in government erodes further. Thus a central task of democratic leadership is to educate citizens in the difference between technical and adaptive work so that they are prepared to entrust public officials who tell them the truth rather than pander when no easy answers are readily at hand.

The normative tests of adaptive work, then, involve an appraisal of the processes by which orienting values are clarified in an organisation or community, and the quality of reality testing by which a more accurate rather than convenient diagnosis is achieved. By these tests, for example, serving up fake remedies for our collective troubles by scapegoating and externalising the enemy, as was done in extreme form in Nazi Germany, might generate throngs of misled supporters who readily grant to charlatans extraordinary authority in the short run, but it would not constitute adaptive work. Nor would political efforts to gain influence and authority by pandering to people's longing for easy answers constitute leadership. Indeed, misleading people is likely over time to produce adaptive failure.

Ronald A. Heifetz is co-founder of the Centre for Public Leadership at the Kennedy School of Government. This essay is adapted fron an entry in the forthcoming Encyclopedia of Leadership, *Sage Publications 2004.*

Notes

1   RA Heifetz, *Leadership Without Easy Answers* (Cambridge: Harvard University Press, 1994), p 76.
2   RA Heifetz and D Laurie, 'The Work of Leadership', *Harvard Business Review* (January 1997, republished December 2001).
3   RA Heifetz and M Linsky, *Leadership on the Line: staying alive through the dangers of leading* (Boston, Mass.: Harvard Business School Press, 2002), ch 1.
4   See E Mayr, *Toward a New Philosophy of Biology: observations of an evolutionist* (Cambridge, Mass.: Belknap Press of Harvard University Press, 1988) pp 127–47.
5   RD Masters, *The Nature of Politics* (New Haven: Yale University Press, 1989), ch 3.
6   Heifetz, *Leadership Without Easy Answers*, pp 30–2.

6. Creating an education epidemic in schools

David Hargreaves

Twenty years after the first wave of national school improvement policies was germinated, we appear to be entering another, relatively rare, period of transition in which the basic parameters of the education reform agenda are once again altering. At the forefront of this change, from the government's perspective, are the Key Stage 3 strategy, covering the 11–14 age range, and the plan for a coherent 14–19 phase, through a series of reforms over the next decade.[1]

These are not just the latest stage in the long road to school improvement, but a significant change in direction. First, the language has changed: 'improvement' has given way to 'transformation'. Second, the government's earlier insistence that standards could be raised without the debilitating distraction of attempting to change institutional structures has been replaced by the conviction that structural reform is now critical, that it has to be radical and be matched by innovation, presumably radical too. There is no explicit strategy for this ambitious programme of innovation; indeed, there is a lurking suspicion that advocating it too loudly might unleash a 1960s wave of anarchic innovation leading nowhere.

At the same time this shift does not mark a return to an approach in which all consequential change in the system arises from the redesign of formal structures by central architects of policy or ideology. What seems to be emerging is a far more open-ended process which seeks to combine action at many different levels of the system in coherent, purposeful ways. The most important characteristics of this process are not yet clear.

The limits of levers

Between 1997 and 2002, the literacy and numeracy strategies in primary schools were among the most impressive of the government's achievements in education. But the rate of improvement has levelled off. The literacy and numeracy strategies were a new top-down, highly prescriptive lever that, despite much early opposition to this undoubted challenge to the professional autonomy of primary school teachers, has on the whole worked, though research is indicating that although teachers like the strategy, the improved results are a consequence of teaching to the test rather than teaching better. All levers have their limits. Educational processes are complex, affected by many variables, so the amount of improvement any single lever can effect is smaller than reformers might wish. Moreover, when a new lever has a demonstrable positive impact, policy-makers tend to push the lever beyond its potential.

Can a more locally determined set of reforms for secondary schools be achieved with as much success, and in a similar time frame of about five years, as the nationally determined strategies for the improvement of primary schools? And might such a strategy be used in several areas of reform, and as a complementary strategy in areas where the top-down, prescriptive strategies are reaching their natural limits? In *Education Epidemic* I argue that such a strategy is possible, and that it might help provide a foundation for system-wide transformation.[2] The pamphlet sets out five essential elements of such a strategy.

Creating the right climate

Innovation will not flourish among practitioners unless they have:

- ○ the motivation to create new professional knowledge
- ○ the opportunity to engage actively in innovation
- ○ the skills for testing the validity of the new knowledge

○ the means for transferring the validated innovations rapidly within their school and into other schools.

This means that government must give active permission to schools to innovate and provide a climate in which failure can be given a different meaning, as a necessary element in making progress.

Disciplining innovation

A school that encouraged every member of staff to innovate in any preferred area, and then provided support for the activity, would squander its efforts on ideas that would rarely turn into transferable applications. Identifying urgent problems to tackle and being able to relate them to the needs of the wider system is therefore essential. This means also that practitioners must be able to compare their innovation against 'best practice', which is far more rigorously and clearly defined than is currently the case.

Transferring innovation through networks

The path to transformation requires every school to be willing to give away its innovations for free, perhaps in the hope of some return, but with no guarantee of it. This is the culture that characterised the beginnings of the internet, which itself started out as a peer-to-peer network of cooperating users. In an education system that consists of schools linked to one another in networks, it should be relatively simple for a school or teacher to get in touch with a peer as a source of best practice, as a centre of innovation, or as a partner – and in any area of educational concern.

Making a learning system

It is not merely schools that must be transformed, but some of the other institutions that serve schools. Their relationships also have to be transformed so that these different communities learn with and from one another. At the heart of this change is the way in which central bureaucracies and policy-makers relate to practitioner and delivery organisations. This change is discussed in more detail below, but one precondition of it is that central bureaucracies must learn to view and understand delivery organisations differently.

Mobilising capital

The last 25 years of school improvement strategies and policies have been based on an input–process–output model of the effective school, one that emphasised the power of the school to make a difference to its students independently of its social and economic conditions. Throughout this time the educational community has depended on a set of descriptive characteristics that acted as indicators of success which – through reform – could be replicated in all schools.

Why are schools successful?

It is now time to question whether this basic organisational framework is still the only, or the best, one within which to pursue the goals of universal education. We need to understand the deeper cultural and structural underpinnings of schools that make them effective. In other words, we need concepts that explain why schools are successful, not merely describe the nature of that success (such as having a culture of achievement, or being well led, and so on). If the same concepts can also be used to explain what makes other kinds of organisations or whole social systems such as cities or societies effective and successful, then the relationship between schools and their wider environment is more explicit.

Schools, like other organisations, are effective to the extent that they can mobilise the range of resources at their disposal in effective and efficient ways. What is the most useful way in which to characterise these resources, which are inevitably of different kinds? And can we devise terms that apply to different categories of organisations and not uniquely to schools? One way is to treat an organisation's resources as various forms of capital: material, intellectual, social and organisational.

Material capital

The most familiar version of capital is material capital. This includes financial capital as well as physical capital such as buildings and equipment, which could in principle be realised as money. All organisations have to manage their material capital; schools are rarely rich in material capital, and in any event it is not always clear who actually owns it.

Intellectual capital

A school's most important resources are its people. So a second form of capital is intellectual capital, which embraces what is usually called human capital, or the education and training of individuals, with a broader spectrum of allied qualities – their knowledge, skills, capabilities, competences, talents, expertise, practices and routines. Intellectual capital is, in contrast with material capital, one of the organisation's invisible assets. Schools are evidently rich in the intellectual capital of the teachers and staff, but also of the students.

Like all invisible assets, intellectual capital is often taken for granted, easily overlooked or even neglected. A school that failed to monitor its budget or audit its accounts systematically and regularly would be considered to be seriously negligent. But a school's intellectual capital, especially among the staff, is rarely monitored and audited. The staff usually know when the school is in debt, and why; but do they know the state of their intellectual capital in the same way? In some areas schools find recruiting high-quality staff difficult and do become aware of a lack of intellectual capital; in the same way, continuing professional development of staff is increasingly seen as an investment in teacher quality, and so serves as an enhancement of intellectual capital. Thus the term intellectual capital is a useful way of bringing together an important set of people resources that are sometimes treated separately.

Social capital

Another of a school's invisible assets is its social capital, a term that covers the character and quality of the social relationships within an organisation. Social capital has cultural and structural aspects. Culturally, it consists in the trust that exists between the organisation's members; structurally, social capital is the extent and quality of the networks by which its members are linked to one another. As applied to a school, social capital refers to the extent of trust between head and staff and among the staff, between staff and students and among the student body as a whole, as well as the extent and quality of the school's internal networks, such as the organisational networks of subject departments and many kinds of informal network among friends. A school that is rich in social capital has a strong sense of itself as a community.

Organisational capital

The fourth and last form of capital is organisational capital, the knowledge and skill that are needed to deploy the organisation's intellectual and social capital to achieve the its goals. That an organisation is rich in material, intellectual and social capital does not automatically mean that these resources will be used properly or fully: the resources have to be actively mobilised and organisational capital is the know-how that is needed to do so. In recent years we have begun to realise that in many organisations, including schools, intellectual and social capital are underestimated and underused, and this is in part because managers and leaders lack the insights and skills that comprise organisational capital.

Effective schools

In effective schools the four forms of internal capital are deployed to good effect. The schools are led in ways that develop and use organisational capital to mobilise in full the intellectual and social capital so that the central goals of the school – student behaviour and achievement – are met. Great school leaders have organisational capital in abundance. They know not only how to deploy the school's existing intellectual and social capital, but also how to increase them. On this view, the primary function of a head is to ensure that as many people as possible have distributed leadership opportunities to increase and mobilise the school's intellectual and social capital. Ideally, the school's management and organisational structures should reflect the optimal distribution of these opportunities to contribute to its overall effectiveness, and to learn from what it already does well. This mobilisation of capital and the knowledge of how to increase it is, quite simply, a measure of the organisation's capacity, especially the capacity to manage change and improvement, processes that demand, and are fuelled by, high levels of social and intellectual capital. This points to another very important aspect to organisational capital, namely the capacity to look outwards to find and exploit the external opportunities for enhancing all forms of capital to supplement the internal resources.

Thus an organisation can boost its intellectual capital by drawing on the intellectual capital of its partners and stakeholders. A school's intellectual capital is enriched by the external capital held by parents, governors, local employers and so on. These same stakeholders can enlarge the school's social capital by providing added trust as well as links into new external networks, local, national and even international. One of the most important forms of organisational capital, especially in the headteacher, is the capacity to convert these external sources of capital into internal capital.

Using the terms intellectual, social and organisational capital provides us with a way of reading across from schools to other organisations and to the community, so that we see how the same underlying forces characterise good schools, good partner organisations (which include many other schools) and good local communities. Internal and external capital are interdependent and often mutually reinforcing. As long as we use very different terms for explaining good schools and good communities, we risk talking about how schools can be improved or transformed as if this could be done independently of stakeholder organisations and the community. This is in defiance of the facts and it can generate inflated expectations of what individual school leaders can achieve alone. If intellectual and social capital can be affected by what we choose to do, in the community and in the school, then there are good grounds for optimism and potential recipes for social improvement, even trans-formation.

The capacity to innovate

High levels of internal capital, in which external capital has also been harnessed, yield high capacity – but to do what exactly? One of the most important forms of this capacity is the capacity to innovate. The mobilisation of intellectual capital fosters new ideas and creates new knowledge that leads to successful innovation in making the school more effective. Such innovation creates new professional practices so that teachers work smarter, not harder. Innovation requires high levels of intellectual capital, which is a necessary but not sufficient condition. Innovation also requires high levels of social capital, the trust between head and staff and among staff to engage in the new practices and risk-taking that are inherent in innovation. Moreover, the social capital also generates the internal networks by which new professional practices can be transferred from one teacher and classroom to another; and the external networks may well be the source or spark of an innovation. In the most effective schools, the best professional practices – which are of course a form of intellectual capital – are not locked inside the heads of a few outstanding teachers and restricted to the privacy of their classrooms: through the knowledge-sharing arising from high levels of social capital they become the common property of all who might profit from them.

An organisation that engages in systematic and regular innovation is, by definition, a learning organisation; where the social capital is strong, it will be a learning community.

The pathway to innovative schools is through investment in the four forms of capital. There is no other route. If schools merely implement innovations that are devised elsewhere and are mandated or imposed on them, they may in some sense be better schools, but they will not be innovative schools and their capacity for innovation may be weakened rather than strengthened.

The four forms of capital capture the 'growth potential' not merely for an individual school but also for the system as a whole. As schools strengthen their external networks all the participants in the networks potentially enhance their levels of intellectual and social capital. Since inter-school networks have to be positively led by committed heads, the sharing among them potentially increases their own organisational capital too. This is why federations and collegiates are potentially important: they require high levels of capital to develop but once under way they generate yet more capital. An education service that consists of autonomous, isolated schools cannot generate additional, shareable capital. In consequence, there cannot be the innovation networks on which the rapid transformation of system depends.

Transforming the central bureaucracy

Transformation of the education system as a whole into a learning system is the most important challenge. At present the talk is of transformed schools, so that central government remains largely as it is but, as a result of government action, in the form of policies and initiatives, the schools experience transformation. In reality, the system is truly transformed when its central bureaucracy is also transformed, itself becoming an exemplar of the learning organisation that it advocates for schools.

Yet the Department for Education and Skills (DfES) as an organisation differs substantially from schools. It is rich in some forms of capital and poor in others. It is rich in material capital, with huge funds at its disposal; but it is weaker than many schools in terms of its intellectual and social capital, as well as the organisational capital among senior officials to mobilise the internal capital that exists in the Department. For the DfES to become a learning organisation and more effective in reaching its goals it will, like the best schools, have to learn how to draw on the high levels of intellectual, social and organisational capital in so many of its 25,000 partner schools. To reach that, the DfES would have to rethink its relationship to schools, and move from a hierarchical, command and control relationship to one with higher social capital, brokering and amplifying the different kinds of network that form the fundamental unit of the new education system.

Restoring trust and encouraging networks as the foundations for an innovative system of secondary education does not mean that the government should leave education entirely in teachers' hands. Rather it is a matter of creating a mix of vertical–central and lateral–local reform strategies that complement each other because they are effective in distinctive circumstances. The DfES has to play a different role in this lateral strategy by:

○ identifying the main areas for transformation and securing collective ownership of them
○ creating a climate of trust among the stakeholders
○ laying down an appropriate infrastructure, both social (networks) and physical (ICT)
○ encouraging schools to use this social capital to mobilise their intellectual capital in innovation
○ enhancing the organisational capital of all school leaders
○ respecting the self-organising systems and spontaneous order within the education service
○ brokering key partnerships to ensure that the process of continuous innovation and knowledge transfer thrives as the hubs change in the light of new themes and priorities for innovation.

In short, the very system over which ministers of education preside has itself to become a more self-conscious and effective learning system in parallel to the learning organisations they advocate at grassroots level. Transformation requires everyone to learn: constantly, openly and quickly.

David Hargreaves is a former professor of education at Cambridge University and a former head of the Curriculum and Qualifications Agency.

Notes

1   For secondary schools, two recent documents, *A New Specialist System: transforming secondary education* (London: Department for Education and

Skills, 2003) and *The London Challenge: transforming London secondary schools* (London: Department for Education and Skills, 2003), chart the way forward.
2   D Hargreaves, *Education Epidemic* (London: Demos, 2003).

7. Developing policy as a shared narrative

Kate Oakley

The majority of public services are delivered at the local level – by local authorities, schools and GPs and increasingly by a dense array of partnerships. Yet for some time central government has believed that the best way to improve those public services has been through national initiatives, rather than the other way round. To take just one example, we have a 'National Strategy for Neighbourhood Renewal'.

Yet the exhaustion of government by targets and the increasing understanding of a need for systemic improvements is going hand in hand with the realisation that if we want to 'renew' neighbourhoods, we need to start by finding out what neighbourhoods want and then work upwards – that way renewal might actually take hold.

As recent Demos work has argued, systemic improvements will only occur when we learn to integrate policy-making with practice on the ground – ending the artificial separation between thinking and doing.[1] But the capacity for this is often lacking. The gradual erosion of local government in terms of functions and funding has stripped out valuable layers of organisational memory and knowledge. Worse still, local political culture is weak.

Third-sector organisations often have a rich understanding of local needs but are paid simply to deliver centrally developed services. Any questioning of government policy leads to fears that contracts and funding will not be renewed. And the many partnership organisations designed to bridge the gaps between sectors often lack the time to develop shared learning before they are expected to 'deliver'.

There are genuine problems with the resource base of local government and the structures that underpin its relationship to central government, but increases in funding or institutional reshaping will not in themselves bring about transformation. We need to create locally responsive, knowledge-rich organisations which have the funding base and the political powers to effect change, but that also, crucially, have the learning capacity to understand those changes and to relate them back to local needs.

This will require a new model of 'local knowledge' and a new confidence in the value of that knowledge. If central government is to be challenged because its policies fail to work at local level, local agencies need to develop their own policy narratives and tell them with clarity and conviction. They need a shared knowledge base, which recognises the validity of hard data and also its limitations. They need to find ways of enriching data with anecdotes and experience. Above all, perhaps, they need to stop looking at their own communities and policy areas through a central government filter.[2]

This is more than an administrative fix. The managerialism that so dominated New Labour's first term has understandable roots, but its consequences have been damaging. One does not have to hanker for the days of stronger trade unions, or Militant-led local authorities, to believe that people are often 'politicised' and therefore educated by conflict and debate. The concentration on 'getting things done' in public service reform often results in a smoothing over of inherent conflict or power imbalances, particularly in partnership organisations. This can mean that the required debate does not happen, those with a minority point of view disengage and learning opportunities are missed. From a desire to avoid what is seen as 'pointless conflict' the life has effectively been drained from some local institutions. A form of 'productive conflict' needs to be reintroduced if we are serious about transformation.

My argument here draws on recent experience in economic development with a number of local and regional agencies.[3] Clearly, there is no simple read across from one policy area to another. What fails in economic development may work well in education or healthcare (for example, the literacy and numeracy hours, or national standards for cancer treatment). But even where national standards and targets are appropriate a local understanding of the impact of these targets, or the best way to reach those standards, cannot be attained without richer local knowledge and critical reflection.

Recognising the barriers to local transformation

The greatest problem hampering local transformation is a lack of self-confidence and belief. This may seem a strange thing to say given the boosterism that accompanies initiatives like Liverpool's Capital of Culture success, or the anticipated revival of East Manchester on the back of the Commonwealth Games. Yet many of the models for these came from elsewhere. Liverpool would love to do what Glasgow did and Manchester points to Sydney, so much so that it often appears that everywhere wants to be somewhere else. This loss of confidence has led to a commodification of ideas about urban renewal and regional development. This is reflected in various trends: the 'cookie cutter' approach, 'projectitis', an increase in partnership working and lack of local accountability.

The 'cookie cutter' approach

One has to spend very little time reading regional economic strategies to despair of the sameness of these documents, with their references to the knowledge economy, their use of sporting metaphors (the Premier League is a particular favourite), the importance of creativity and so on. My point here is not to question the argument that the UK is moving towards a more knowledge-intensive economy, or that the knowledge economy will have a major impact on all of Britain's regions – but to question why the nature of that impact where it affects particular cities or regions is so poorly understood. All areas of the country, whatever their industrial base, human capital stock, scale or history are discussed in these documents as if they are identical and as if a knowledge economy will eradicate their differences, instead of exacerbating them, overnight.

This problem is particularly apparent when talking to local officials. One colleague tells the story of arriving at a consultancy briefing on creative industries to be greeted by a client sitting with five copies of *The Rise of the Creative Class* on their desk, the best-selling book by US regeneration guru Richard Florida. The implicit message was 'now give us one of these please'. By uncritically adopting national and international discourse without reference to local context, policy-makers can lose the ability to recognise the distinctiveness of their own regions and the issues they face.

During recent work in the Black Country, an area of the UK where small and often low-skill manufacturing firms make up a major part of the economy, I was repeatedly told, 'What this area needs is a research-based university like Cambridge.' No recognition was made of the fact that a sudden wave of Cambridge-style graduates is unlikely to be absorbed by Black Country firms. Rather than trying to understand the difference between the knowledge economy of the Black Country and that, say, of the South East of England, we seem hell-bent on trying to replicate a single model of the knowledge economy across the country. Everywhere is said to need a research university, some incubators and a 'creative hub', preferably with a sprinkling of cafés, galleries and fancy shops. All regions are pursuing the same economic development strategy, despite the evidence that their human capital stock cannot support it and that they will have difficulty attracting or retaining the kind of workers on which these economies depend.

'Projectitis'

The short-term nature of many projects means that organisational learning is often not effectively picked up and absorbed. The use of consultants (mea culpa) is often seen to exacerbate this, but there is no reason why this should be the case. The problems with public sector research and consultancy are generally less to do with the quality of the consultants employed and more to do with the lack of a framework into which such knowledge can be placed. If there is no shared understanding, then individual pieces of informally commissioned research have nowhere to fit and will fail to make a collective impact.

Partnership working

The complexity of some social issues has led to an increased emphasis on partnership working. While few would question the need for this, the weight of expectations on partnerships to 'join up' policies at the local level can often be unrealistic. Partnerships are formed by groups of people from different sectors, with unequal powers, who usually bring with them different baggage in terms of expectations and understanding. Yet despite this diversity, they are rarely allowed time to develop a common narrative or set of assumptions. Partnership members often lack a common language or knowledge base. Local officials might describe the problems of a local economy as 'a lack of NVQ 2s', while local employers talk of not getting enough staff 'with the right attitude'. Policy types refer to evidence of a stronger economy as 'improvements in Key Stage 1–4', while local residents see it as 'fewer cheap shops'. Despite its simplicity, one instinctively leans towards the second description, not because the first is inaccurate, but because the second at least suggests that someone is paying attention to their local area.

Structures of accountability

Where money and ideas come from the centre, accountability is often directed back to the centre, so the space for local innovation remains constrained. This is particularly noticeable in regional development agencies (RDAs), which have no local political legitimacy. In place of this, we have an insane competition, where RDAs vie on a national stage to make the most exaggerated claims about their 'world class' or 'Premier League' ambitions. One longs for just one region to claim it would be content with 'mid-table respectability', a decent quality of life and low unemployment.

Creating a new political culture

If we want to develop the policy-making capacities of local agencies, we need a smarter political culture that does not exclude those not versed in public sector acronyms. It is not that we don't need evidence, it is just that the nature of that evidence needs to be broadened out, and its limitations understood. In developing such a culture we need to be less afraid of conflict, more open to disagreement and more willing to support an initial learning process. Let me suggest three steps towards this: develop a shared narrative through joint learning; develop a common knowledge space and common language; and set up local think tanks or research organisations.

Develop a shared narrative through joint learning

The Mayor of London's Commission on the Creative Industries was set up by Ken Livingstone in January 2003 to identify ways of improving the competitiveness of creative industries in London. The Commission, which was made up of 15 representatives from the creative industries, business, policy and education, met for some five months, during which it heard evidence and arguments from a wide variety of sources. The 'evidence' presented was a mixture of theoretical models, examples of best practice and case studies drawn from the UK and abroad. While much was made of specially commissioned research on issues like black and ethnic minority involvement in these sectors, much of the learning actually took place in informal conversation, in site visits to successful projects and in the forum for debate and discussion that the Commission ran.

Much of what the Commission heard was anecdotal – practitioners reporting on their experiences in getting premises or finding funding. But by listening to people with genuine experience (sometimes of 20 years or more), by providing a supportive forum for debate and, above all, by learning together as a group, the Commission went on to develop a shared narrative, which reflected the process of change and learning that they had been through.

The constraints of funding are unlikely to allow each health action zone or community partnership the same space to learn, but more learning opportunities clearly need to be built into the development of local partnerships. Expert testimonies, case studies and visits to sites are absolutely vital as a way of enhancing capacity.

Develop a common language

We need to develop a common knowledge space and a common language. This can be done in a variety of ways, from formal 'observatories' that bring together evidence across a variety of fields, to the development of local economic models, or even the collection of personal testimonies and oral histories. The important thing is to recognise that any complex field is likely to require a mixture of formal data and informal knowledge and that the aim of any model, observatory or database should be to promote dialogue, not to be revered as the source of all wisdom.

There will undoubtedly be tensions between the views of different partners and decisions have to be taken about what evidence to use in particular instances. For example, school league tables have often been criticised for not capturing what local people value about their school – its atmosphere, or its role in the community. This is not to suggest that local, informal knowledge should always be privileged over official statistics. Many people may value their local hospital because they find the staff friendly, but if its rates of recovery from surgery are worse than other hospitals, this needs to be taken into account.

Finally, we need to be aware of the limits to 'evidence'. Some data simply does not exist and some questions are impossible to answer in the form people frequently require – such as the 'economic impact' of culture, or the 'social value' of participation. Dealing with this is a matter of expectation management and of conviction. For example, the 'evidence' that free entry to museums broadens access is questionable; but it is unlikely to narrow access and it enhances the experience of those who do choose to visit museums. So just do it.

Setting up local think tanks or research organisations

This is particularly valid at a regional level, where greater strategic policy-making capacity is needed. Many RDAs are developing observatories (on the economy, culture or the environment), but too often these are used in 'delivery' mode to back up decisions already taken by central government, rather than as tools for debate.

What is needed are more bodies charged with critical thinking about the implications of policy at the local level. The North West Development Agency has recently set up a think tank to comment on its strategy for creative industries, a model that could be replicated by other RDAs. Criticisms of the 'thinness' of the policy culture outside London often fail to take account of the vast range of community groups, lobbying organisations, trade unions and so on that exist in any region, but it is fair to say that the formal structures linking these to public agencies are often weak or ad hoc. Local think tanks could provide this link.

Conclusion

No amount of shared learning is going to make up for the fact that at local level you need real political power, backed up by funding, if you are to create genuine democratic and institutional renewal. Local responsiveness can only work if agencies are held to account locally – if the Black Country were to develop a different model of its knowledge economy it would be of little use if this resulted in its central funds being withdrawn for producing too many nurses and not enough bio-engineers. Challenges and alternatives to centralised thinking can only come from deeper local knowledge. We just need to let it breathe.

Kate Oakley is associate director of the Local Futures Group and a Demos associate.

Notes

1   D Chesterman, *Local Authority? How to develop leadership for better public services* (London: Demos, 2002).
2   For a discussion of the structural reasons for this, see A Amin, D Massey and N Thrift, *Decentering the Nation: a radical approach to regional inequality* (London: Catalyst, 2003), www.catalystforum.org.uk/pubs/index.html.
3   Particularly my work with the Local Futures Group for the Black Country Consortium and the London Borough of Camden.

8. Local government
the adaptive tier of governance

Barry Quirk

The pressures on politicians from a hyper-demanding citizenry match the pressures for public service improvement from consumers. People want better, quicker and cheaper public services; and they want public institutions and politicians to be more responsive, more sensitive and more accountable to their increasingly diverse needs and concerns. These twin pressures for change – for more personalised and efficient public services and a more responsive politics – permeate all tiers of governance.

Such pressures require a high level of adaptive response from public institutions and politicians. Generally, adaptive responses are characterised by being more attuned to changes in environmental context than conventional command-driven change management approaches. Change that is shaped by, sensitive and appropriate to the dynamics of context is the opposite of the institutionalism underlying the current orthodoxy, in which public institutions are in thrall to their own intrinsic needs and bureaucratic demands and act principally to capture public value for their own purposes of growth and sustenance.

By contrast, adaptive approaches start with the context of customers, citizens, clients and communities and not the content of organisational strategy. At face value, this implies heavy reliance on a 'living systems' or naturalistic approach to policy implementation. But it would be a fallacy to apply the blind logic of natural systems evolution to the purposive management of change and progress in the world of human affairs and organisational change.[1] Instead, public policy must use adaptive approaches to render public institutions more sensitive to their context and more appropriate in their delivery of purposive change. Their aim is to turn institutions outward in order that they can better transform their operating context.

In this piece I argue that the local tier of government offers the best prospects for successful responses to these enormous pressures. This is not because solving problems locally is the easiest or the most convenient – it is simply where solutions to persistent problems and continuing under-performance are most likely to be discovered.

The nature of change

We all know that technology changes at a pace far swifter than our ability to adapt our own behaviour (how fast can you text message?), let alone that of our organisations (how many staff in large organisations have truly flexible work arrangements supported by modern communication technologies?). However, social and economic changes occur in an even more complex and differentiated manner. Some social changes seem driven by our greater economic interdependence and connectedness – by the impact of greater flows of money and people across the world. Other changes appear to reflect relative social and cultural insularity. Some communities remain characterised by relative social homogeneity while others experience increasingly radical diversity, not simply of ethnic origin, but of culture, family composition and household type.

Another key feature of social and economic change is that it is highly reflexive in character – the changes impact on themselves and therefore tend to accelerate, redouble or further complicate the underlying or precipitate change. This is why we need to beware the seduction of simple solutions; usually a tangled web of causation underlies complex problems such as differential patterns of employability, ill health or criminal behaviour.

Whatever their provenance, the predominant pressures for change are not simple, predictable, linear and synchronous. Even those with simple origins have become horribly complicated over time through the multiple interactions of people and institutions. For in social policy and organisations, complicated problems (which are difficult to solve) often develop into complex problems that may only just lie with the domain of the soluble – placing a premium on pragmatism of politics and practicality of management. Understanding the diverse and complex nature of these pressures for change is therefore the first step in improving the effective performance of public services and in regaining public confidence in the trustworthiness of public institutions.

Purposeful adaptive responses

In these circumstances, conventional 'command and coordination' approaches by public organisations (adopted to imitate the industrial production model of organisation developed in the late nineteenth century) now appear inadequate over anything more than the very short term. It is only really feasible to command actions (before the event) when the external environment for action is highly ordered and predictable – a relatively uncommon feature in public service.

Increasingly, 'experts' tasked with specialist roles within large organisations are self-organising and operate collaboratively across organisational boundaries in professionally styled 'communities of practice'. Maths teachers, neuro-surgeons, planners and auditors each work for a single institution but they seldom owe their sense of personal purpose and mission to one institution – more usually they have diffuse loyalties to the public, their client, their professional community and their employer. They therefore seldom operate only in the context of strict hierarchical coordination mechanisms within organisations.

The need to shift from a governing dynamic of mutual adjustment and informal cooperation to one of planning, control and impersonal authority has usually been viewed as being a function of scale and numbers. Consider the case of driving. In small numbers, there is simply a need to mark the road and leave well alone (drivers' deal with each other through a process of 'tit for tat' cooperation); with rising numbers of motorists and road intersections, the impersonal authority of traffic lights becomes necessary. And at some point when negative externalities of traffic begin to weigh heavily against the positive personal value of mobility through car usage, road pricing and restricting mobility shifts swiftly into consideration.[2] In fact, I would argue that adaptive approaches are more apposite when the number of cases and interactions are very high. Mass-scale systems need new learning capabilities if they are to offer services differentiated on the right basis; adaptive approaches are necessary for such learning to occur.

But if adaptation requires an overarching moral purpose, then public organisations need to be adaptive to their context not simply to succeed as organisations but to enable them to transform the context in which they operate. Their aim may be to improve the public value of their services, to increase fairness and justice or to enhance the quality of life of their client group. Adaptive approaches are the means for a progressive end. Schools do not adapt to the circumstances of their pupils in order to succeed as schools; rather schools need to be adaptive to local circumstances in order for the pupils to be more able to succeed in life. It is this purpose beyond the institutional boundary that demands that schools, healthcare institutions and local authorities should be adaptive.

The morphology of public service reform

Private sector competition helps to drive continuous innovation in products and services, in the process keeping apace of the underlying dynamism of society at large.[3] In the public sector, the institutional traditions and character of delivery (based around schools, hospitals, local councils and other public agencies) requires a complementary impulse to ensure their continuing and dynamic relevance to wider society. To date this impulse has been through various reforms initiated by national government. The quasi-market approach of the late 1980s and early 1990s gave way to a more centrally directed approach to experimentation by the first term Labour government.

This was subsequently overtaken by a more considered approach based on strategic service planning and service programme delivery in the second term. This latter approach is based on a firm belief that delivery involves a drive to improve performance overall as well as ensuring that differential performance between agencies is narrowed through the converging influence of applying 'best practice' techniques to service delivery. The agenda is now focused on how best to apply the principles of public service reform to heighten the overall impact of the considerable investment now being made in key public services.

However, too frequently there is conflation at the heart of the public policy debate: the fusion of 'service performance' with 'social problems'. Patterns of ill health are not the same as patterns of variance in hospital performance, and neither are patterns of skill levels the same as patterns of variance in school performance. This is not to argue that variance in school and hospital performance is irrelevant. Tackling poor service performance requires effective managerial attention and effort; tackling persistent social problems requires much more than effective public service management – it requires a whole system approach (involving citizens, politicians, and service providers alike).

In the context of a plan-based approach to public service delivery, the diverse and complex character of social and economic change presents enormous problems of prediction and control to politicians and public managers. Intuitively we know that the future is unknowable but instinctively we are driven to control it! We would never believe anyone who said they could tell us whether it was going to rain the Thursday after next; and yet we seem desperate to attend conferences to listen to experts forecasting medium-term social and economic trends.[4]

Whether our forecast is based on pretended fore-knowledge or conjecture, the recurring theme for political leaders and public managers is that public action requires prior consideration and deliberation in the public domain. So in the public sector our conjecture as to 'what might work' becomes tested in the light of public debate – prior to, during and then after implementation! That is why all public agencies need to build a public legitimacy to act – delivery involves citizens, it is not simply done to them. More often than not public service issues require mediation between competing claims or differing interests. Different voices and perspectives are evident in most public interest questions: in the contest over the development of land; in the recombination of services between health and social care; in the wider community use of local schools; and in the demands for increased investment in recycling our refuse.

In the design of services to solve today's problems and the anticipated issues for tomorrow public agencies need therefore to engage people from all communities. And to act as public guarantor of fairness and justice (a key purpose of state action) they specifically need to take full account of those people with least power and resources at their own disposal.

Levels of adaptive response

At the national level one key issue is how best to systematise and incentivise adaptive responses by government departments or sub-national governmental agencies. Quite regularly over the past decade or so successive governments have used, to varying success, fiscal rewards and penalties to encourage shifts in institutional behaviour. The local public service agreements, where local councils agree to heightened targets on a series of agreed national and local priorities in return for a 'performance reward grant', are perhaps the most recent attempt to construct a coherent compact between central and local government. These local public service agreements, sponsored by HM Treasury, the Office of the Deputy Prime Minister and the Local Government Association, are now maturing into a 'second generation' round focused on achieving adaptive responses locally to national policy priorities.

At the local level many local councils have recognised the need for whole-system approaches to solving local problems and one-half of all 'top tier' local councils have been evaluated as providing good or excellent services to their local population.[5] From the citizens' perspective adaptability is required at five levels:

○ *the adaptive worker* where customer interaction is focused on providing value to the customer and is not rigidly bounded by the parameters of the worker's task role and job definition

○ *the adaptive team* where a team of workers have complementary skills and talents that are delivered in combination to provide added value flexibly (with project-focused teams being the most adaptive)

○ *the adaptive service* where service is designed with a view to diversity in demand, with a mixed economy of provision, a variety of service strategies (balancing risk in implementation by 'not putting all eggs in one basket') and personalised customisation in operational delivery

○ *the adaptive organisation* where social and environmental diversity are embraced and where internal and external organisational boundaries are irrelevant to the design and delivery of services

○ *the adaptive locality* where agencies in a local area work collaboratively to provide new combinations of value to changing patterns of citizens' needs.

Effective local councils have invested in adaptability – politically and organisationally. They are alert to the dynamics of local civil society and are attuned to the changing demands of local political life. They have faced the truth that local political parties need continually to be grounded in local concerns and issues of public interest rather than being consumed by the decision needs of the town hall. They have questioned their own democratic legitimacy and in some cases, such as Lewisham, have moved to systems of direct election for mayors as local political leaders.

Organisationally, effective local councils have adopted an outward-facing approach where managers are expected to act as civic entrepreneurs, raising the value of community life through the quality of local public services (whether directly provided or partnered with the private sector). Effective local councils have a pervasively purposeful 'can do' culture where political leaders seek to animate their communities and public managers seek to generate a sense of urgency and progress in their organisations.[6]

Perhaps more generally, effective local councils have actively invested in organisational agility.[7] Specialist expertise is increasingly necessary but rigid professional boundaries or functional alignment (the dreaded 'departmentalism') is a poor excuse for organisational inflexibility. Public institutions (like local councils) can enhance their organisational agility in a number of ways; they can make use of:

O   'co-production' approaches with citizens or consumers
O   technology (mobile devices, palm-top computing, collaborative software, and so on)
O   external partners in the public sector (their facilities, assets and people)
O   partners in the private sector (their access to expertise and capital)
O   'interim or seconded' management or staff to increase capacity to act.

Just one example of the adoption of organisational agility by local councils is the investment in tools and practices to enable flexible working among field staff. Increasingly mobile data and communication devices are being integrated into the daily working of a wide range of staff – from car parking enforcement staff to child protection workers. This investment in agility is sensible – it makes local councils more effective. But citizens want whole systems to be adaptive, not just single institutions. And it is here where effective local government has the potential to act as the adaptive tier of government.

Adaptive responses in local systems

There are numerous examples of how local responses to social problems demonstrate combined adaptive approaches from a range of local public institutions and actors. Admittedly several of these have occurred because of the strength of external sponsorship of specific interventions (as with Sure Start early years programmes in deprived communities). However, many local responses have emerged spontaneously through effective cross-agency working at the operational level: in health and social care; in school-based community development; and in estate-based action to tackle crime. Four examples merit illustration.

Tackling crime through local crime reduction partnerships

First, tackling crime through local crime reduction partnerships (led by local councils) is a good example of how local councils and the police force have devised adaptive operational responses to local circumstances. It is possible to cite many examples where action-oriented problem-solving has occurred in multiagency and multidisciplinary settings to combine efforts and target action on issues such as street crime, hot spots for vehicle crime, residential burglary, persistent young offenders and so on. Generally, the approach is to examine local factors in the context of national crime reduction priorities and targets and then to devise operational strategies across agencies for tackling local priorities, local offenders and local offences. The point is that these adaptive responses require local councils and police force to share operational responsibility for a local 'wicked issue' and then to share public accountability for tackling it together.

Improving pupil attainment in schools

Improved pupil attainment across the school system is another example of where local councils can act as catalysts for change beyond institutional boundaries. Local education authorities are increasingly acting to establish educational pathways across the age cohorts and across institutions (schools, colleges and so on) as a complementary strategy to their efforts to improve school effectiveness. The development of a broad but targeted curriculum offer for the 14–19 year age range is one of several approaches where at the local level the approach to increasing adaptive responses by public agencies goes beyond institutional boundaries.

Cross-agency working in health and social care

The continuum of care between traditional social services provision and healthcare is rich with examples of adaptive practice by professionals seeking to improve the quality and effectiveness of public services. Incentives for collaborative working are again a strong pressure for adaptive change. For example, the issue of hospital 'bed blocking' used to be a big problem for patients, their families and for health and social care staff. Now people are usually discharged from hospital with suitable care quickly and more appropriately. They do not stay in hospital any longer than is necessary, and long stays can increase their exposure to infection and compound their health problems. These changes in practice were triggered by externally imposed targets and a mix of fiscal rewards and penalties; but although these played a crucial part in the change, the substantive changes in practice would not have happened without local ownership and widespread professional commitment to implementation.

Similarly, in mental health services local practitioners – social workers, nurses, psychologists and psychiatrists – have led the way in developing local community mental health teams. These multidisciplinary teams provide a single point of access and an integrated service for people with serious mental health problems. They are adaptively arranged around needs rather than professional boundaries. People whose care needs previously fell in the interstices between services and who are more likely be readmitted to hospital are increasingly being supported by community mental health work.

Local strategic partnerships

Finally, over the last three years and in some 90 or so of the most deprived local authority areas, local councils have developed local strategic partnerships (LSPs) involving constituent partners from the public sector and the private sector together with community representatives. These LSPs tend to be led by locally elected politicians (directly elected mayors or leaders of local councils) and they offer a genuine prospect for encouraging whole system responses locally. Each LSP is charged with developing its own local community strategy, which could act to catalyse the adaptive responses on a concerted basis of constituent partner agencies at the local level.

Encourage cooperative styles of working

Without effective local leadership, multiagency and cross-sector working can so easily descend into win–lose, zero sum games across institutions. Moreover, the complex nature of the issues and problems being addressed can lead to collaborative inaction and inertia through 'too much knowing and not enough doing'.

Adaptive responses require cooperative styles of working between front-line workers across organisations and between professionals within organisations. The sources of cooperative endeavour have been subject to considerable research and theory over the past 20 years,[8] although there has been little attempt to link this emerging body of work with management practice. It is clear that cooperation needs to be encouraged between individuals and between groups of individuals. It should not be left to chance.

In local councils we need to devise personal work incentives and appraisal systems that encourage cooperative working at various layers – for senior managers, for professionals and for front-line workers. Incentives need to be devised that encourage cooperation between, say, two management executives with different but overlapping or interconnected operational responsibilities. Cooperation does not simply emerge through invocations for public spirited altruism or the natural process of joint working – people need to be taught the benefits to them of reciprocal behaviour with others.[9] Moreover, it may be useful to examine how to encourage cooperation between, say, neighbouring local councils, through wider systemic incentives in politics and funding.

Conclusion

From a central government perspective it often seems that local public institutions adapt national policy aims to their own local resource needs and purposes. To dampen this perceived internalised institutional bias, the government have developed considerable process controls, such as national performance indicators, and a thorough framework of institutional inspection. This may serve to converge public management practice around an acceptable norm (or towards an ideal type) or more pessimistically it may become distorted into an overelaborate process of pseudo-controls.[10] The government and the key inspectorates appear alert to the dangers of this second route; the implication is that transformation in public services demands excellence in local leadership – to build agility, pragmatism and flexibility into the design of organisations and to build alliances with citizens, public and private sector partners as well as employees and their trade unions.

This means that local political leadership is pivotal to the adaptive capacity of public services as a whole, and that it must be intertwined with equally excellent administrative and professional leadership. Adaptive leadership is about 'making happen what would otherwise not happen':[11] seeing the possibilities and opportunities to solve the real problems that face real people. And that is the real deal. Local leadership is adaptive because the problems being addressed are not theoretical. At the front line, local leaders do not invoke change, they generate it. The local tier of government is the adaptive tier because it operates at the level where things have to get done. It is the tier of governance where politicians and public managers need to focus on the discipline of operational delivery; it is the tier where real and persistent social problems are unavoidable and seek urgent resolution; in short, it is the tier where the science of the deliverable meets the art of the soluble.

Barry Quirk is chief executive of the London Borough of Lewisham.

Notes

1   R Dawkins, *A Devil's Chaplain* (London: Weidenfeld & Nicholson, 2003).
2   K Arrow, *The Limits of Organization* (New York: Norton, 1974).
3   G Hamel, *Leading the Revolution* (Boston, Mass.: Harvard Business School Press, 2000).
4   P Medawar, *The Strange Case of the Spotted Mice* (Oxford, Oxford University Press, 1996).
5   Audit Commission, *Patterns for Improvement* (London: Audit Commission, 2002).
6   C Leadbeater, *The Man in the Caravan and other Stories* (London: Improvement and Development Agency, 2003).
7   R Ashkenas et al, *The Boundaryless Organisation* (San Francisco, Calif.: Jossey-Bass, 2002).
8   R Axelrod, *The Evolution of Co-operation* (New York: Basic Books, 1984).
9   E Sober and D S Wilson, *Unto Others* (Cambridge, Mass.: Harvard, 1998).
10 C Hood, 'Public sector managerialism onwards and upwards or "Trobriand cricket" again?', *Political Quarterly* 72, no 3 (2001): 300–9.
11 R Pascale et al, *Surfing the Edge of Chaos* (London: Texere, 2000).

9. Towards the learning society?

Riel Miller[1]

The next phase of 'public sector reform' is not about managerial innovations. It is about the creation of new communities, new networks and new markets. It is about redefining what the public sector does rather than how it does it. This does not mean that the management of the services currently provided by public employees should not be reformed. As with all management, public or private, it is crucial to upgrade and improve organisational effectiveness continuously. But the more profound question, one that concerns what politics is about, is what kind of society people want and how to get there.

Regardless of political stripe, the long-standing challenge facing governments in OECD countries has been how to turn the potential for much greater freedom into a reality.[2] Of course the context within which people exercise their freedoms differs according to distinct national histories, predilections and values. Some, for example, accept greater income inequality and environmental pollution, others do not. But in all cases the aspiration is to go beyond the condition of freedom as liberation from oppression or want to freedom as the capacity to define, express and fulfil one's self. Not the imaginary 'self' as monad. This is a political fiction that is now as credible as the twentieth-century fantasies of a perfect command economy or perfect market. For humans the 'self' is inherently social, defined through and with reference to the 'others' that surround us. Our degrees of freedom tend to coincide with the sophistication of our interdependence.

This is why taking freedom, and the responsibilities that always go with it, to the next stage is the fundamental and most difficult political task. It has never been easy to improve our capacity, individual and collective, to establish and sustain ever more freedom-enhancing social orders. Breakthroughs have never been quick or painless. Old habits and entrenched power structures die hard.

Whole societies do not jump from one way of being to another. Real revolutions, as demonstrated by the failed experiments of the twentieth century, are only the outcome of gradual, incrementally radical reforms that build up the new around the old. As Washington Irving observed long ago in his fable about Rip Van Winkle, the radical nature of the American revolution's historical break was made evident because Rip went to sleep a subject of his Majesty, George III, and woke up 20 years later 'a free citizen of the United States of America'.

Change may be a constant, but not all change is of the same order or import. There are long periods of consolidation or incremental and continuous improvement. During the latter half of the twentieth century, refinement of accepted methods and conventions was the primary attribute of change, sustained by the success of the mass-consumption, mass-production mixed economy and the stark fears induced by the Cold War's balance of terror.

As we move into the twenty-first century, many of these bets are off. In part this explains the high profile and sense of urgency surrounding current efforts at reform. The possibility of radical change to the context in which people live demands that the next stage of public sector reform must address the opportunity that may currently exist to reframe the basic conventions which structure daily life.[3]

What if politics is successful?[4]

What if politics is successful in moving OECD societies to the next stage of freedom? The overriding characteristics of such a society are diversity and creativity. Why? Because this time around the goal is

Figure 3 Time–space flexibility, diffusion of authority and knowledge

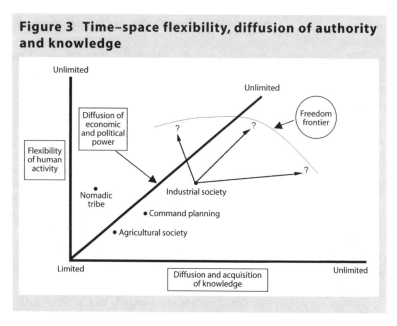

the capacity to use freedom to express one's self rather than ensuring liberation from the constraints imposed by the struggle for subsistence. This shift helps to explain why demand for the goods provided by public services is never static, and why what people want increasingly revolves around the ideas of flexibility and personalisation. One way of helping to imagine such a shift is to use a 'possibility space diagram'.[5] Figure 3 illustrates three important dimensions of change in people's freedom: the amount of time–space flexibility they have, the diffusion and acquisition of knowledge and the diffusion of economic and political power.[6]

Time–space flexibility

The first dimension of change is the degree of time–space flexibility available to people in their everyday activities. Surviving off the land, punching the clock at the factory gate or signing in at the office tower leaves little room for flexibility in when and where one works and lives. Industrial societies make up for this time–space rigidity with relatively open labour markets, which introduce flexibility through job turnover. We adjust our lives to fit the when and where of work. One future possibility is much greater and more efficient interdependence, making it possible for people to choose when and where they work and live. Around the clock and around the world, the availability of collaborators and trusted communities could create an unprecedented degree of time–space flexibility in people's daily lives. This is a big step.

The diffusion and acquisition of knowledge
The second variable is the diffusion and acquisition of knowledge. Out at the frontier of the possibilities evoked by Figure 3 it is imaginable that knowledge transparency improves to the point that it underpins much greater space–time flexibility; networking moves to another level of complexity and spontaneity; and interconnection and interdependence evolve to become even more complex and differentiated. There are many intractable obstacles to such universal transparency: inadequate communication skills, crude intellectual property rights, the lack of indexing standards for the internet, labyrinthian payment systems and the difficulty of validating people's claims to a particular competency.

Nonetheless, it is possible to imagine politics succeeding in overcoming the entrenched interests of the industrial era, which are busy defending most of these barriers. Pushing all the way out to the frontier, where the costs and benefits of knowledge diffusion and acquisition are fully transformed, even opens up the possibility of moving beyond industrial-era technocracy towards new 'open-source' forms of specialisation. Breaking the centuries-old hold of guilds (professions) and certifiers (universities) on specialised knowledge would be radical change indeed.

The diffusion of economic and political power
The third dimension of change is the diffusion of economic and political power. A basic historical undercurrent continues to erode

hierarchical, autocratic power. During the industrial era the struggle for representative democratic institutions and human rights have already produced dramatic advances. For large parts of humanity the arbitrary and absolute rule of father, husband, cleric, boss, lord or politician has been significantly reduced. The challenge now is to try to imagine the attributes of taking this diffusion of power to the next stage. The temptation is to think of revising constitutions, reforming the functioning of legislatures, or rewriting the rules for corporate governance. These are certainly worthwhile tasks. But they fall into the same category as improved management.

In contrast, at the edges of the possibility space power flows easily where and when it is needed to accomplish tasks. Grasping what this might mean is easier when we think of time–space flexibility and knowledge diffusion, since discretion over when and where we do things and ready access to knowledge are familiar concepts. Though still far off in many respects, we can begin to imagine conditions where the decision-making power needed to determine the shape of social and public goods would become a function of people's unique needs and circumstances. This, albeit from a long distance, is what the emerging ideal of personalisation may look like.

Understanding the obstacles

From today's perspective it is not surprising that it is difficult to imagine how economic and political power might flow freely, in ways that allow for real-time reallocation depending on the task at hand. Indeed most of the attributes of the freedom frontier illustrated in Figure 3 seem well beyond current decision-making practices and capacities. How would such fluid power, living and knowledge systems work? Are we really willing to give up our tried and true methods for such uncertainty?

No doubt the same kinds of questions have plagued parents and political leaders when confronted with children and followers who want to break with the past. It is hard to let go, and few institutions or generations do so voluntarily. Perhaps the most critical obstacles to overcome are those that limit learning. Learning is the key source of the capacities needed to grasp and exercise greater freedom. The conditions determining the capacity to learn will be central regulators of the pace and direction of long-term change.

Looking at OECD countries today, individuals and institutions seem ill equipped to carry the burden of creativity and self-direction that would characterise everyday life at the frontiers of Figure 3. Achieving this level of differentiated interdependence certainly requires much more than simply re-engineering or transforming the supply side of service-providing institutions.

Personalisation, by definition, means direct involvement in the production process by what we still call the consumer. Such co-creation poses a significant challenge to many of the fundamental distinctions of the industrial era, especially that between supply and demand.

Treating supply and demand as separate phenomena has shaped the way organisations are conceived, designed and managed. It structures and limits our thinking about markets into fields of action and reaction. It parallels the heretofore powerfully productive division of labour between conception and execution. It is engrained in notions of worker obedience and shopper passivity. In effect, the stunning success of mass-era approaches to loosening the constraints of subsistence have become among the greatest obstacles to fostering diversity, creativity and flexibility. Mass production depends on uniformity and reducing complexity. Mass consumption depends on acceptance and reaction. Public service institutions like schools, despite much rhetoric to the contrary, continue to cement key expectations and behaviour patterns that have more to do with being punctual and listening to the teacher than discovering self-governance and creativity.

The challenge then is to move beyond the prefabricated and homogeneous solutions of the mass era. Lest this seem too daunting, it is worth recalling that we have been here before, on the cusp of a period of transition. There are precedents for phases of change marked by 'radical incrementalism' such as the decades of transition from rural–agricultural to urban–industrial societies. Humans have the capacity to shift the focus of their innovative nature from the refinement of what works in a relatively stable system to searching for new solutions in an emergent system.[7] This is what our rather short span of evolutionary success rests on.

What can governments do?

What can governments do to facilitate twenty-first century transitions towards freer, more creative societies? The overriding theme is improving people's capacity to learn in order to reach better decisions. How?

One approach is to take advantage of the composite nature of transformation. This means searching for the experiments, successes and failures, at the margins, outside the mainstream as a way of discovering what works. But if the aim is to harness complexity and diversity to meet human needs then the image of what works will be more like the swirling of a kaleidoscope than the hard edges of a blueprint. Succeeding amid this kind of indeterminacy calls for a disturbingly big change to the ways in which we currently try to reduce risk and its perception, away from simplification and total control towards cultivating the full use of all available information.

Fortunately, this may be easier to achieve than our industrial era reflexes lead us to believe. The internet is only the most recent and obvious example of how a few simple rules that allow a network to function can underpin an explosion of activities as heterogeneous as they are impossible to predict. Networking is what it is all about. Generating a virtuous circle of incremental radicalism capable of producing positive change across whole societies requires the simultaneous development of many new networks.

Two examples illustrate ways in which governments could forge ahead with the next wave of reform by facilitating the emergence of new networks of networks. These new systems could become as central as the feudal marketplace once was and the school and firm still are.

Cybercitizenship

Past advances in freedom and responsibility were closely connected with bloody struggles for citizenship rights. Not long ago the worst punishment available to the sovereign was banishment – which for all practical purposes meant denying a person an identity – revoking their point of social belonging, their vouch for. The development of the modern nation staked out a territorial boundary for the right to citizenship and the obligation, usually tacit, to accept and abide by a set of minimum and uniform values and behaviours. Tomorrow's freedom goes beyond these boundaries. Getting there will require new ways of asserting one's identity and living with the consequences.

At the moment the need for new approaches to identity is mostly illustrated by negative efforts to cope with the failure of existing methods. For instance, according to the American Federal Trade Commission, 27.3 million Americans have been victims of identity theft over the last five years and the costs in 2002 were over $50 billion.[8]

Considerable concern is also being expressed about the problem of controlling identity in airports and at border crossings (not to mention more clandestine migration). At the same time, invasion of personal privacy is a growing concern. Then there is the tidal wave of viruses, Trojan horses, worms and spam that undermine the effectiveness and transparency of the internet.

Many efforts are under way to fix these problems, so far without too much success. The bigger worry is the lack of a positive, coherent approach to the vacuum of trust which currently limits the potential of communication and exchange based on electronic networks. The biggest cost is not the direct cost of identity theft, but the opportunity cost in creativity and wealth foregone. Without a common basis for trusting a vendor on the net or a person at an airport neither networks nor nations can function effectively.

Setting up trust infrastructures that can efficiently and legitimately provide cybercitizenship will involve overcoming a range of hurdles from technical ones related to biometrics and cryptography to political ones like oversight and accountability. But by establishing the right to a trusted identity, safeguarded by law and under the control of the individual, more widespread freedom and creativity could become genuinely viable.

Validating what people know

We know that firms are engaged in massive efforts to manage knowledge, which largely means people, and governments are striving very hard to encourage people to learn continuously. But so far not much progress has been made in clarifying the value of human capital either for organisations or for individuals, both of which need to decide where and how to invest in knowledge and learning. A large part of this failure stems from the inadequacies of the near-universal credential systems we currently use to ascertain whether or not people are competent to do a job.

It was recently reported in one OECD country that one in three curriculum vitae contains false credentials. If most of what counts as successful performance can be learned on the job, this is not a major problem, as long as the individual is capable of learning. But in a system where work collaboration is far more spontaneous, diverse and fluid, across a vast network of interdependencies, it is far more serious.

The award of knowledge credentials through qualifications suffers from rigidity, uniformity and conflicts of interest, whereby awarding institutions have a strong interest in excluding sources of learning other than their own, while individuals have an equally strong interest in overstating their achievements and capabilities.

Overcoming this conflict calls for a new independent institution able to provide a politically legitimate and trusted keyword search index to all available human know-how; in the process it would allow people to find and trust suppliers, collaborators or 'experts' for any task they might be preparing to undertake. In contrast with today's approaches such a system will not depend on a static or uniform definition of skills, since in different places and at different times the attributes of a particular competency change.

Establishing a universal system for validating what people know should not be any harder than, for instance, the difficult and protracted setting up of an efficient and sustainable financial sector. Methods of accounting, safeguarding, evaluating and exchanging, physical and monetary assets did not appear overnight. Nor will human capital banking.

Back to managerial reform? Towards experimentalism!

There are many other examples where the time has come to nurture the periphery and experiment with new formulas and institutions. Intellectual property rights in music and pharmaceuticals are two. Payment systems and rules for safeguarding the transparency and seamlessness of our information networks are two more.[9]

Such problems create concrete opportunities to nurture incrementally radical changes that could move us towards long-term transformation. Small-scale experiments that are the seeds of tomorrow's dominant conventions are all around us. The greatest difficulty, particularly for political and policy leadership, is finding the threads of coherence amid this flux, and learning to recognise the patterns of an emergent system. Today the imperative is to avoid failure at all cost. This is understandable given the way risk was managed in the industrial era – through engineered, predesigned and tested certainty. If something failed then you were a failure. But in a learning society the idea of picking only the winning initiatives is a contradiction in terms.

Governments cannot force coherence on social and organisational systems characterised by complexity and diversity. What collective activities such as governments, firms and families can do in order to encourage transformational change is to follow a few key principles that improve the ability to find security in complexity rather than uniformity:

- o Seek out and encourage experiments – learning by doing. This is about being able to value and learn from failure and success.
- o Understand that in most cases the means are the ends.

Only the values associated with specific outcomes can be anticipated in advance. In general, the values embodied by outcomes cannot be produced by means that are antithetical to those values.

O Search for new metrics and new standards that can enable the transparency (a common base for diversity) and trust (accountability) that makes networks flourish. Here the challenge is to tease out the collaborative and competitive dimensions. Networks depend on solidarity when it comes to key rules while at the same time giving rise to the differentiation that spurs conflict. Much experimentation and learning is still needed before we ascertain the best ways to sustain the balance.

This is not an exhaustive list; discoveries about how to do things differently are being made all the time. Governments, through their reform agendas, should aim to encourage such discovery, enhance the capacity of public servants and systems to learn from them, and look for the patterns and conflicts that point towards coherence in the future shape and character of existing and new public institutions. Done well, such strategies could make the difference between whether society achieves radical transition or not, and whether it takes us towards greater freedom without provoking too violent a backlash.

Riel Miller is a specialist in long-term strategic thinking and principal administrator at the Centre for Educational Research and Innovation, OECD, Paris.

Notes

1   Thanks to Tom Bentley for invaluable encouragement and insight. The views expressed in this chapter are the personal opinions of the author (email: rielm@yahoo.com).

2   See A Sen, *Development as Freedom* (Oxford: Oxford University Press, 1999) and T Bentley and D Stedman-Jones, *The Moral Universe* (London: Demos, 2001).

3   For a detailed exploration of the possibility, not probability, of radical change over the first few decades of the twenty-first century see the OECD

International Futures Programme's 21st Century Transition series, available at www.oecd.org/dataoecd/12/42/1903212.pdf. Also see M Storper, 'Conventions and institutions: rethinking problems of state reform, governance and policy' in L Burlanaqui, AC Castro and H-J Chang (eds) *Institutions and the Role of the State* (Cheltenham: Edward Elgar, 2000) for a discussion of changes in the conventions that order everyday life.

4   Note that this scenario of what life might be like 'if politics is successful' is based on the learning society scenario developed using a 'possibility space' methodology. See R Miller and T Bentley, *Unique Creation – Possible Futures: four scenarios for schooling in 2030* (Nottingham: National College for School Leadership, 2003), available at www.ncsl.org.uk/mediastore/image2/possible-futures-flyer.pdf; and OECD International Futures Programme's 21st Century Transition series, available at www.oecd.org/dataoecd/12/42/1903212.pdf.

5   Ibid.

6   Also see R Miller, 'Why measure human capital?', in Panorama, AGORA V, *Identification, Evaluation and Recognition of Non-formal Learning*, CEDEFOP, Thessaloniki, March 1999, available at www2.trainingvillage.gr/etv/publication/download/panorama/5132_EN.pdf.

7   B Goodwin, *How the Leopard Changed Its Spots: the evolution of complexity*, (Princeton: Princeton University Press, 2001).

8   See www.ftc.gov/opa/2003/09/idtheft.htm.

9   R Miller et al, 'The Future of Money', in *The Future of Money* (Paris: OECD, 2002).

10.Public value

the missing ingredient in reform?

Jake Chapman

Public value has been defined as 'what the public values – what they are willing to make sacrifices of money and freedom to achieve'.[1] This is a self-obvious definition, but it also makes clear that the notion of public value, and any uses that might be made of it, are going to challenge the territory normally dominated by economics. It would be counter-productive to attempt to establish public value in opposition to, or as an alternative to, traditional economics. However, a comparison between the two approaches does help to clarify what public value has to offer.

It is also obvious from the definition that public value has a lot to do with politics. Political processes exist precisely to make sense of what the public values and to translate this into decisions about laws, budgets and policies. One of the central ideas underlying the concept of public value is that government and public institutions do not just use resources such as capital and labour, which have alternative uses, but also make use of a unique resource, namely the power of the state to compel. The ways in which this unique resource is to be used is not the same as the way in which other resources are used. So while it is appropriate for markets to determine how capital and labour and natural resources should be used, the way in which the power of the state should be used is determined by a different process. It is determined by collective decision-making, as expressed through democratic procedures and institutions. One of the assertions made by those advocating the use of public value is that wherever the power of the state is being exercised, then the most appropriate criteria for decision-making is public value.[2] This theme will be picked up at various points in this article.

A richer view of the individual

One of the key distinctions between a purely economic approach and a public value approach to public services is the way in which individual members of the public are regarded. Within economic theory the public are regarded as consumers, expressing their individual preferences in their actions and purchases. This focus has been incorporated into new public management (NPM) as an emphasis on public choice – with the commensurate use of league tables for schools and hospitals. The view of the public from the public value perspective is much richer. From a public value perspective individuals have a number of different roles with respect to public services, roles that an individual will switch between depending on the context.

These different roles can be illustrated by considering how an individual may regard the services she receives from a local hospital. The first and most obvious role is that of a consumer of the services on offer – and this is the same as the role presumed within economics. However, imagine for a moment that the individual arrives at the hospital and finds that it is dirty, that she is kept waiting before being able to explain her requirements to anyone, and when served she is treated rudely and without respect. Under these circumstances the person is not simply a dissatisfied customer of the services; as a citizen and tax-payer she is also upset that the standard of provision is so low. Had she experienced something quite different – an extremely plush waiting room with free coffee and tea provided, a receptionist able to deal with her requests obligingly and immediately – she might also have been disturbed at the high level of service her taxes were paying for. So as the source of finance for the service, she wants it to be neither too meagre nor too plush. These are quite distinct from her reactions as a consumer (which is unlikely to be critical of the plush quality of service).

There is another role as a citizen in which our hypothetical visitor to the hospital is interested. It matters to people as citizens not just how well they are treated, but also how well others are treated. Broadly within the provision of public services we as citizens require an equable treatment of all, the young and old, the rich and poor. This requirement for equity and fairness has no counterpart in markets.

Finally, our citizen and consumer discovers that in terms of the outcome of her visit to the hospital, she has a significant role as a co-producer. She is not just a passive receptor of health services but is actively engaged in determining her own health through a myriad of significant decisions – what to eat, whether to exercise, what to drink, whether to smoke cigarettes and so on. This is true of most public services; the outcomes depend as much on the actions of citizens as on the activities of the service providers.

So when considering public value it is necessary to regard individuals as:

○ consumers of the services provided
○ citizens requiring that their taxes are spent appropriately
○ citizens with an interest in issues of equity and fairness
○ co-producers of the outcomes associated with the services provided.

For each of these roles the feature of the service that contributes to value is different, and it is this multidimensionality of value that provides a rich way of thinking about public services. It is actually not sufficient for individuals to know that their child is going to the best school: they also want the general standard of state education to be high and available to everyone, not just to those who live in middle-class suburbs. In this sense the publication of school league tables can contribute to the destruction of public value.

Restoring trust, ensuring sustainability

There are other dimensions of public value that have not been elucidated by the hospital example. What the public values is a combination of outcomes, services, security and trust. Issues of security and trust are dependent on the relationship between government and citizens and it is this aspect of public value that has been neglected by the focus on service provision. Indeed, promising to improve services to meet some new target, such as reduction in waiting time or class size, and then not meeting the target leads to a reduction in trust and public value – even though the service level itself may have increased.

Trust is an important dimension of public value, all the more so because over recent years the general level of trust in government and public institutions has declined. It is also a dimension that appears irrelevant if the focus is entirely on 'delivery' and 'targets' – which results from regarding people as simply consumers of public services and not also as citizens.

Another aspect of public value not captured well by the hospital example is that of sustainability. As a citizen I do not want to see an improvement in waiting lists achieved by some short-term fixes that cannot be sustained, such as sending patients to be treated in another country. What I want to see is a development of the entire system of provision so as to produce a lasting improvement in the service, including its quality, its ability to treat me with integrity and to treat everyone fairly.

The final dimension of public value I wish to draw attention to is the degree to which a policy or way of providing a service conforms to the broad conceptions of a just, liberal civic society. A strategy for reducing crime that resulted in more innocent people being jailed would destroy public value, as would a strategy for reducing hospital waiting lists by denying treatment to certain classes of people. Much of the objection people have to the ways in which government makes use of 'spin' and media presentation is that it undermines their trust in government and how they expect the government of a liberal society to behave.

A new agenda for public value

So public value is a multidimensioned construct, which aims to capture what it is that the public value in relation to the government's use of the power of the state. Public value is increased when:

○ the level of service provision is improved
○ the quality of service is increased, particularly in treating all recipients with respect
○ the equity or fairness with which the service is delivered is increased
○ the service provision is more sustainable and takes into account the needs of future generations
○ the provision of the service is done in a way consistent with the expectations of a liberal civic society
○ the service provision enhances the level of trust between government and citizens.

Theoretically it is possible for economics to include all these factors in its analyses, but in practice it is extremely difficult and contentious and tends not to be included in the economic evaluations of policies. But there is another distinction between economics and the approach based on public value, and this hinges around the concept of public preferences.

Conventional welfare economics accounts for value in terms of individual self-interest and personal preferences that are taken as given and not amenable to change by policy-makers. Individual preferences are aggregated into a 'social objective function' and the role of policy is to ensure resources are used to achieve these objectives as efficiently as possible. However, there are aspects of public preferences that are not captured by such an approach – aspects in addition to the omissions listed above.

One important aspect of public preferences is that they may be dependent on other people's behaviour and preferences. These interdependent preferences are common in areas of public services – as, for example, people's willingness to use public transport depends on other people's support and willingness to use it. Another aspect is that part of the role of government is to shape these public preferences. They are not be regarded as fixed or given, but amenable to change through the provision of new options and arguments. Finally, it is important to note that there is no ready-made process whereby individuals can register their views and preferences on a wide range of public-service-related issues. There is no device, such as a price mechanism, to aggregate the preferences of individuals, so it is part of the function of government actively to seek to understand and identify public preferences and how they may change over time.

In his book Mark Moore proposes that all public sector managers should operate so as to increase the public value generated by their organisation.[3] He suggests that this is not a matter of passively responding to public preferences, but of actively seeking out ways in which the power of the state can be used to create public value. This is in stark contrast to the generally accepted view of public managers as administrators ensuring that organisational capacity is provided to deliver a prescribed programme. Moore argues that even when public managers have a mandate, there is usually sufficient ambiguity and compromise built into the mandate to provide room for manoeuvre. Furthermore, by determining how a policy is to be implemented, and by controlling the information related to the programme, the manager has a great deal of discretion. Moore argues that it would be better to have the manager use this power and flexibility openly in pursuit of public value rather than covertly behind a mask of servitude.

So what difference would using public value make in delivering public services? It is hard to predict in detail how such a radical change of approach might develop, but there are a number of obvious consequences:

○ If public value is accepted as the primary objective of government in delivering public services then it becomes critically important for departments and agencies to discover and understand exactly what it is that the public wants.

○ The design and evaluation of policies becomes more complex and multidimensional. This does not require more advanced calculus but greater creativity and sensitivity in devising policies. It also means that the predominance of value currently attributed to simple service provision is substantially diluted.

○ If public value is the gauge by which government is itself judged then it also needs to be the objective given to departments and agencies operating on its behalf. It would be quite inappropriate to construct targets on the basis of public value, but with hindsight judgements can be made about which agencies and policies created and which destroyed public value. (This parallels the way in which private companies are judged by their profitability – which is always assessed after the event.)

In the transition from the welfare state to the regulatory state, which took place in the late 1970s and early 1980s, there was a clear shift of emphasis away from public services in favour of private consumption. Governance, however implemented, has continually to balance the public good, as represented by communal services, institutions of civic society and collective welfare, with the preferences, choices and freedoms of individuals. Within the welfare state there was a clear predominance of the requirements of collective and public goods, within the regulatory state the dominance was reversed and favoured individuals and private choices. As each set of needs is met by the new form of governance so there is a growing demand for attention to the neglected component. It is clear that the pendulum is now swinging back towards concern for public services. It is not accidental that the reputation of the current government hinges on its ability to deliver what the public wants in terms of public services. This is why public service reform needs to embrace a much wider conception of what the public wants, which is precisely what the public value concept provides.

Jake Chapman is a systems expert and author of the Demos pamphlet, System Failure: why governments must learn to think differently.

Notes

1   Cabinet Office, *Creating Public Value: a new framework for public sector reform* (London: Cabinet Office, Strategy Unit, 2002), available at www/strategy.gov.uk/2001/futures/attachments/pv/publicvalue.pdf. www.number-10.gov.uk/su/pv/public_value.pdf. The current article leans heavily on this exposition of public value and the reference below.

2   MH Moore, *Creating Public Value* (Cambridge, Mass.: Harvard University Press, 1995).

3   Ibid.

11. Technology enabling transformation

Robert Watt

The government has set an ambitious agenda for public sector reform. The focus is now on delivery and it is clear that information technology will play a significant part in this. Now, more than ever, there is intense scrutiny of any new public sector IT projects, coming as they do against the backdrop of some high-profile procurement failures. It is increasingly clear that the standard centralised and inflexible IT solutions of the past cannot serve the needs of a constantly changing and developing public sector. One size doesn't fit one – let alone all. As Jake Chapman argues individual autonomy and the widespread use of communication technologies constrain control from the centre. Historically, IT has been a rather blunt instrument of change, a way of automating existing services in a one-off 'big bang' with a lack of effective central control the 'big-bang' can compound the problems in transforming services not alleviate them.

However, the latest technology allows different types of changes to be implemented at different times and in different ways. In Hewlett-Packard (HP) they call this 'adaptive infrastructure' because it allows the IT systems of an organisation to adapt to changes in structure, management and services as quickly as decisions are made.

Why is this important? Effective change management has become a critical success factor in the private and the public sectors. For private sector companies, it is about responding to the changing demands of customers whose expectations are being shaped by globalisation, diversity, individualism and new forms of communication. In the public sector there is a need to respond not only to the more assertive demands of the public – the users of the service – but also to politicians and officials facing proliferating policy demands and greater public scrutiny.

Rigid command and control structures are being forced to give way to public services based on complexity, flux, unpredictability and diversity. These new services are non-linear, evolutionary, informal, networked and autonomous, making design and delivery very difficult to manage. What is crucial is the ability of public sector organisations to learn and therefore adapt, especially to unintended and unforeseen consequences that increasingly determine outputs. This requires trial and, yes, error – but error at a small, localised scale. Risk cannot be eliminated but it can be better managed. Coping with constant service change will rely on renewal and transformation from within, rather than external change being forced from without. Adaptive public services will increasingly demand an adaptive IT infrastructure.

The HP story

For HP, this 'change agenda' has been crucial. In 2002, Hewlett-Packard merged with Compaq to create the largest IT company in the world. It was the largest ever technology merger and created some huge business and logistical problems for the company's own service framework. Their experience of clients allowed them to develop a new type of IT infrastructure for the new company. This new 'adaptive infrastructure' is one that can grow and develop IT resources in line with the growth and development of the rest of the company. As the merger bedded down, it allowed business management decisions to be made and implemented in response. The infrastructure became a key enabler of change.

In merging its systems with those of Compaq, HP created a single communications network, linking more than a quarter of a million PCs and handheld devices, and handling around 26 million emails a day. Their adaptive infrastructure model has enabled HP to cut the number of software applications used across the company from 7,000 to 5,000, and to cut the number of different components bought by the company from 250,000 to 25,000. After one year, HP had cut US$3.5 billion in annual costs – a billion dollars more and a year earlier than promised to shareholders at the time of the merger.

For HP's global operations, an infrastructure that had central standards and connectivity was essential, but so too was the ability for local subsidiaries to manage their own change in ways that met local conditions. The adaptive model provided this support, and there are interesting parallels to the way government is looking to deliver locally accountable public services.

What is 'adaptive infrastructure'?

Essentially, adaptive infrastructure offers a new paradigm for IT resourcing, based on a networked approach. Previously, IT infrastructure had either to move ahead of the development of an organisation, as a large and sometimes unnecessary expense, or to follow on behind the organisation's needs, thereby acting as an inhibitor of growth. By contrast, an adaptive infrastructure develops in a modular way, growing as service change requires. Key modules within this adaptive infrastructure include resource virtualisation, management, flexible working methods and security.

Resource virtualisation

Virtualisation allows all data centre resources to be pooled together and allocated to services and applications as needed. As priorities change or sudden demands arise, resources can be reallocated by scaling up automatically. This improves service performance and use of resources.

Management

A key component of HP's adaptive infrastructure is the ability to pool assets across departments. This helps organisations maintain service levels by reallocating assets dynamically as and when required to meet performance needs.

Flexible working methods

The development of mobile and pervasive computing environments that support the worker in the field are key to adaptive infrastructures. Technologies such as the digital pen, which allow workers to capture information digitally without changing their work practices, enable transformation with little risk. Handheld computing devices such as the iPaq can be used to modernise services at the point of delivery.

Security

Security is built in to an adaptive infrastructure, through a centralised platform for security implementation across the widest number of applications and system devices. This provides the most effective method for implementing the highest level of security at every level of the architecture, for centralised and distributed applications.

The value of adaptive infrastructure

Like the tap in the kitchen, which can be turned on or off as required, new forms of utility computing combine adaptive infrastructure's resource virtualisation with its adaptive management model. Utility computing can dramatically reduce the operational cost of systems management. Any reallocation of resources can be done with the click of a mouse. Once wired, infrastructure can be reconfigured flexibly and dynamically with minimum effort to respond quickly to changes in policy, new service initiatives or peaks in demand. The total cost of ownership is reduced dramatically through automation, standardisation, simplification and improved use of resources.

For any large organisation the implementation of an adaptive IT infrastructure can help increase efficiency through better use of resources. However, the overriding benefit of an adaptive infrastructure in public services lies in its ability to link IT infrastructure to the changing objectives of the organisation – this is as true in the public sector as in business.

For the public sector the adaptive approach can:

○ tighten the link between it and wider policy objectives; public agencies can anticipate and respond rapidly to new service requirements

○ rapidly and cost-effectively enable development of new services and delivery channels across the widest number of individual departments and agencies

○ increase control over multi-technology environments, through centralised and consolidated services and resources; best in class solutions can quickly be adopted and spread

○ simplify the management of complex, multi-tier systems with a single point of support and responsibility, maximising the productivity of the overall systems environment

○ integrate, develop and consolidate new joined-up services, and manage and extend existing legacy applications

○ consolidate legacy applications on to utility platforms providing a secure, future-proof environment for legacy data and services

○ accommodate utility computing platforms to provide computing on demand for a wide range of central and local applications

○ change and adapt as demand requires or as public services evolve over time; it allows departments to shift and load-balance resources so that they can meet sudden shifts in computing needs

○ provide a 'pay-per-use' model in which the user only pays for additional resources when they are used, thus providing greater control of costs and longer-term planning.

The roadmap to adaptive infrastructure

Central to the approach of adaptive infrastructure is that it works with change as a constant rather than as a one-off. This is crucial for the public sector as IT projects become larger and ever more complex.

A common criticism of some public sector IT projects is that by the time they have been completed (after what seem to be inevitable delays) the systems introduced are already out of date. To avoid these problems in future, HP have developed a 'roadmap' for the transformation of IT systems to a more adaptive infrastructure. This roadmap minimises risk, as change is introduced incrementally. The key steps are described below.

- O *Stabilise* The initial stage is to stabilise the existing infrastructure, ensuring that established business goals are met. Security and business continuity systems are reviewed to ensure that the required level of integrity and reliability is achievable.
- O *Assess* An assessment of the agility of the existing infrastructure is made against defined metrics:
  - O *Time* How quickly can the organisation react to change?
  - O *Range* How far can change reach across the organisation?
  - O *Ease* How easy is it to deploy change, especially in terms of resource or investment costs?
- O *Consolidate* The next step is the consolidation of key elements of infrastructure, such as servers and data storage, to improve the use and efficiency of existing resources.
- O *Virtualise* In the final phase, resources are pooled and virtualised, allowing for applications to be supported as demand or priorities dictate. Use of resources can be monitored, allowing for the internal billing of users and effective management of resources.

The demand for adaptive public services

It is not difficult to find examples of agile public services that will need to be supported by adaptive IT infrastructures. Take the Child Trust Fund (CTF), part of the Treasury's 'Savings & Assets for All' initiative announced in April 2001. In simple terms, the CTF aims to ensure that all children have a savings 'nest egg' to support them into adulthood. The individual funds for each child are likely to be managed by private financial services companies, so it is likely that the administration of the CTF will require a significant IT system. This system will need to be able to track a variety of variables including who is entitled to the fund, who is the adult responsible for administering the fund, how additional government payments can be made and which private sector provider is managing the fund. It will be desirable for some elements of the administration to be joined up with other government systems – such as the birth and death registration system and the 'NHS numbers for babies' scheme. It would also need to be linked up to the systems of financial services companies to allow them to keep the cost of administering the accounts to a minimum.

Although these factors all point towards a substantial IT system, there are a number of ways in which the CTF may develop that could require even greater functionality from the system. For example, the Fund may link into education and training grants, allowances and fees, with the CTF being used to receive student grants, loans, bursaries, or even to pay university tuition fees. Indeed, the CTF could become a new type of individual learning account, receiving government funding for education, training and skills development. Similarly, it is possible that the CTF may be required to link into programmes such as Sure Start, or to have a link with disability benefit in order to help those most in need. Development of the CTF could even be linked in to government grants provided to key workers to help them purchase houses in the South East and other high-demand areas. For any of these wider applications, a flexible, scalable IT infrastructure would be essential, making it an ideal candidate for the application of an adaptive infrastructure solution.

As public sector IT projects become larger in scale, the importance of an adaptive infrastructure will become increasingly evident. Another example would be the Integrated Care Records Service (ICRS), which is a major plank of the NHS's National Programme for

IT. There is no doubt that ICRS will develop and evolve over time in as yet unforeseen ways.

The dilemma facing government is how to secure an effective balance between systems of public administration that are agile and innovative, that provide decentralised and localised flexibility, and yet at the same time maintain purpose and progress consistent with central policy objectives. Breaking out of the 'cookie cutter' or one-size-fits-all appraoch identified by Kate Oakley inevitably leads to tensions in the spaces between the centre and the periphery, between creativity and control. The application of adaptive IT to adaptive public services can help government to strike the right balance. A centrally controlled IT pool can offer support and empowerment to innovation and experimentation on the periphery – perhaps securing the best of all worlds.

Robert Watt is business development manager for HP's public sector division.

DEMOS – Licence to Publish

THE WORK (AS DEFINED BELOW) IS PROVIDED UNDER THE TERMS OF THIS LICENCE ("LICENCE"). THE WORK IS PROTECTED BY COPYRIGHT AND/OR OTHER APPLICABLE LAW. ANY USE OF THE WORK OTHER THAN AS AUTHORIZED UNDER THIS LICENCE IS PROHIBITED. BY EXERCISING ANY RIGHTS TO THE WORK PROVIDED HERE, YOU ACCEPT AND AGREE TO BE BOUND BY THE TERMS OF THIS LICENCE. DEMOS GRANTS YOU THE RIGHTS CONTAINED HERE IN CONSIDERATION OF YOUR ACCEPTANCE OF SUCH TERMS AND CONDITIONS.

1. **Definitions**
   a **"Collective Work"** means a work, such as a periodical issue, anthology or encyclopedia, in which the Work in its entirety in unmodified form, along with a number of other contributions, constituting separate and independent works in themselves, are assembled into a collective whole. A work that constitutes a Collective Work will not be considered a Derivative Work (as defined below) for the purposes of this Licence.
   b **"Derivative Work"** means a work based upon the Work or upon the Work and other pre-existing works, such as a musical arrangement, dramatization, fictionalization, motion picture version, sound recording, art reproduction, abridgment, condensation, or any other form in which the Work may be recast, transformed, or adapted, except that a work that constitutes a Collective Work or a translation from English into another language will not be considered a Derivative Work for the purpose of this Licence.
   c **"Licensor"** means the individual or entity that offers the Work under the terms of this Licence.
   d **"Original Author"** means the individual or entity who created the Work.
   e **"Work"** means the copyrightable work of authorship offered under the terms of this Licence.
   f **"You"** means an individual or entity exercising rights under this Licence who has not previously violated the terms of this Licence with respect to the Work, or who has received express permission from DEMOS to exercise rights under this Licence despite a previous violation.
2. **Fair Use Rights.** Nothing in this licence is intended to reduce, limit, or restrict any rights arising from fair use, first sale or other limitations on the exclusive rights of the copyright owner under copyright law or other applicable laws.
3. **Licence Grant.** Subject to the terms and conditions of this Licence, Licensor hereby grants You a worldwide, royalty-free, non-exclusive, perpetual (for the duration of the applicable copyright) licence to exercise the rights in the Work as stated below:
   a to reproduce the Work, to incorporate the Work into one or more Collective Works, and to reproduce the Work as incorporated in the Collective Works;
   b to distribute copies or phonorecords of, display publicly, perform publicly, and perform publicly by means of a digital audio transmission the Work including as incorporated in Collective Works;
   The above rights may be exercised in all media and formats whether now known or hereafter devised. The above rights include the right to make such modifications as are technically necessary to exercise the rights in other media and formats. All rights not expressly granted by Licensor are hereby reserved.
4. **Restrictions.** The licence granted in Section 3 above is expressly made subject to and limited by the following restrictions:
   a You may distribute, publicly display, publicly perform, or publicly digitally perform the Work only under the terms of this Licence, and You must include a copy of, or the Uniform Resource Identifier for, this Licence with every copy or phonorecord of the Work You distribute, publicly display, publicly perform, or publicly digitally perform. You may not offer or impose any terms on the Work that alter or restrict the terms of this Licence or the recipients' exercise of the rights granted hereunder. You may not sublicence the Work. You must keep intact all notices that refer to this Licence and to the disclaimer of warranties. You may not distribute, publicly display, publicly perform, or publicly digitally perform the Work with any technological measures that control access or use of the Work in a manner inconsistent with the terms of this Licence Agreement. The above applies to the Work as incorporated in a Collective Work, but this does not require the Collective Work apart from the Work itself to be made subject to the terms of this Licence. If You create a Collective Work, upon notice from any Licencor You must, to the extent practicable, remove from the Collective Work any reference to such Licensor or the Original Author, as requested.
   b You may not exercise any of the rights granted to You in Section 3 above in any manner that is primarily intended for or directed toward commercial advantage or private monetary

compensation. The exchange of the Work for other copyrighted works by means of digital file-sharing or otherwise shall not be considered to be intended for or directed toward commercial advantage or private monetary compensation, provided there is no payment of any monetary compensation in connection with the exchange of copyrighted works.

c If you distribute, publicly display, publicly perform, or publicly digitally perform the Work or any Collective Works, You must keep intact all copyright notices for the Work and give the Original Author credit reasonable to the medium or means You are utilizing by conveying the name (or pseudonym if applicable) of the Original Author if supplied; the title of the Work if supplied. Such credit may be implemented in any reasonable manner; provided, however, that in the case of a Collective Work, at a minimum such credit will appear where any other comparable authorship credit appears and in a manner at least as prominent as such other comparable authorship credit.

5. Representations, Warranties and Disclaimer

a By offering the Work for public release under this Licence, Licensor represents and warrants that, to the best of Licensor's knowledge after reasonable inquiry:

i Licensor has secured all rights in the Work necessary to grant the licence rights hereunder and to permit the lawful exercise of the rights granted hereunder without You having any obligation to pay any royalties, compulsory licence fees, residuals or any other payments;

ii The Work does not infringe the copyright, trademark, publicity rights, common law rights or any other right of any third party or constitute defamation, invasion of privacy or other tortious injury to any third party.

b EXCEPT AS EXPRESSLY STATED IN THIS LICENCE OR OTHERWISE AGREED IN WRITING OR REQUIRED BY APPLICABLE LAW, THE WORK IS LICENCED ON AN "AS IS" BASIS, WITHOUT WARRANTIES OF ANY KIND, EITHER EXPRESS OR IMPLIED INCLUDING, WITHOUT LIMITATION, ANY WARRANTIES REGARDING THE CONTENTS OR ACCURACY OF THE WORK.

6. Limitation on Liability. EXCEPT TO THE EXTENT REQUIRED BY APPLICABLE LAW, AND EXCEPT FOR DAMAGES ARISING FROM LIABILITY TO A THIRD PARTY RESULTING FROM BREACH OF THE WARRANTIES IN SECTION 5, IN NO EVENT WILL LICENSOR BE LIABLE TO YOU ON ANY LEGAL THEORY FOR ANY SPECIAL, INCIDENTAL, CONSEQUENTIAL, PUNITIVE OR EXEMPLARY DAMAGES ARISING OUT OF THIS LICENCE OR THE USE OF THE WORK, EVEN IF LICENSOR HAS BEEN ADVISED OF THE POSSIBILITY OF SUCH DAMAGES.

7. Termination

a This Licence and the rights granted hereunder will terminate automatically upon any breach by You of the terms of this Licence. Individuals or entities who have received Collective Works from You under this Licence, however, will not have their licences terminated provided such individuals or entities remain in full compliance with those licences. Sections 1, 2, 5, 6, 7, and 8 will survive any termination of this Licence.

b Subject to the above terms and conditions, the licence granted here is perpetual (for the duration of the applicable copyright in the Work). Notwithstanding the above, Licensor reserves the right to release the Work under different licence terms or to stop distributing the Work at any time; provided, however that any such election will not serve to withdraw this Licence (or any other licence that has been, or is required to be, granted under the terms of this Licence), and this Licence will continue in full force and effect unless terminated as stated above.

8. Miscellaneous

a Each time You distribute or publicly digitally perform the Work or a Collective Work, DEMOS offers to the recipient a licence to the Work on the same terms and conditions as the licence granted to You under this Licence.

b If any provision of this Licence is invalid or unenforceable under applicable law, it shall not affect the validity or enforceability of the remainder of the terms of this Licence, and without further action by the parties to this agreement, such provision shall be reformed to the minimum extent necessary to make such provision valid and enforceable.

c No term or provision of this Licence shall be deemed waived and no breach consented to unless such waiver or consent shall be in writing and signed by the party to be charged with such waiver or consent.

d This Licence constitutes the entire agreement between the parties with respect to the Work licensed here. There are no understandings, agreements or representations with respect to the Work not specified here. Licensor shall not be bound by any additional provisions that may appear in any communication from You. This Licence may not be modified without the mutual written agreement of DEMOS and You.